Cabrillo

*For all the authors
whose books opened
the world to me.*

Cabrillo

*First European Explorer
of the California Coast*

*written and
illustrated by*
Nancy Lemke

EZ Nature Books • *1991* • *San Luis Obispo*

Library of Congress Cataloging in Publication Data:
Lemke, Nancy, 1949-
  Cabrillo: First European Explorer of the California Coast
  Written and illustrated by Nancy Lemke.
  Includes bibliographical references and index.
  1. Cabrillo, Juan Rodríguez, d. 1543. 2. Explorers—America—
Biography. 3. Explorers—Spain—Biography. 4. California—Description
and travel—to 1848. I. Title.
E125.C12L46 1991   970.01'6'092—dc2   [B]   91-32745
ISBN 0-945092-19-9

Design By Nancy Lemke

Published by EZ Nature Books
Post Office Box 4206
San Luis Obispo, California 93403

Acknowledgments

I'd like to thank the following experts for reading my manuscript and checking its accuracy: Craig Arnold of the San Diego Maritime Museum, Dick Cunningham of the Ventura Maritime Museum, and Barry Joyce and Jim Nauman from Cabrillo National Monument. Without the recommendation of Tricia Takacs of the Cabrillo Historical Association, I would not have had the pleasure of creating this book, and without the continued support, flexibility, and constructive feedback of publisher Ed Zolkoski, it would not have been a pleasure. Victor Wild gave me a halo, while graphic design friends Lorena Reyes, Paula Taft, and David Quattrociocchi provided design support. Writing friends Olin Hughes and Leslie Trook gave invaluable encouragement, editing, and commiseration, while my husband, Bob, was patient, supportive, and there for me throughout the project. Thanks to them all.

A Note on the Illustrations

Many of the illustrations in this book are adapted from drawings made by Aztec picture historians—people whose job it was to record daily life and events of merit in the Aztec empire. Assembled by Spaniards into books known as codices, these simple yet informative pictures provide a rich source of images of Aztec life and the Spanish conquest.

Contents

Preface

If you're not from California, chances are you've never heard of Juan Rodríguez Cabrillo. If you are from California, you've probably seen his name on banks, hospitals, schools, streets, even a bowling alley, but do you know who Cabrillo was? If you don't, you're not alone. Cabrillo is frequently referred to as a man of mystery. The unknowns about his life often outweigh the knowns.

For example, no one knows where he was born or when. Was he Portuguese or Spanish? Historians disagree. He first turns up in historical records as a teenager in the New World. How did he get there and why? We don't know. He died during the voyage for which he is remembered, but his burial site is unknown. Even his exact name is debatable. Was it Juan Rodríguez Cabrillo, João Rodrigues Cabrilho, or just plain Juan Rodríguez? Historians disagree.

Fortunately, records do indicate Cabrillo's whereabouts during much of his adult life, verifying his involvement in some of the most spectacular and hair-raising events of the first half of the 16th century.

After Columbus discovered America in 1492, the New World beckoned to adventurers—people willing to risk their lives for gold and glory on the unknown continents. Cabrillo was among the elite of this group—a conquistador—a special breed of men who ruthlessly swept through the Americas claiming all they found for God and Spain. Cabrillo was with Cortés during the conquest of the Aztecs, and he was a trusted captain of Pedro de Alvarado, battling the natives of Honduras and Guatemala. As a seasoned soldier and man of the sea, he commanded a daring voyage of discovery and became the first European to explore the California coast.

Taking the limited facts we have about Cabrillo and placing them against the rich backdrop of his time in history, a portrait begins to emerge. It's not complete, but at least an outline of the old conquistador is visible.

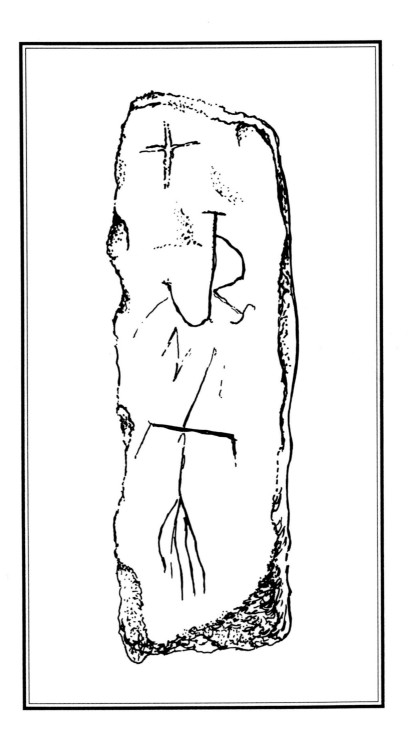

Prologue

In 1901, off the coast of southern California, archaeologist Philip Jones found a sandstone slab on one of the windswept Channel Islands. A little larger than a brick, it had been used by natives for grinding seeds. Lichens encrusted the stone, but an inscription was still visible. Jones gave the stone a brief note in his journal, saying it bore "an incised design on one side." Then he gave it, along with the other things he'd found, to a museum where it was placed in storage and forgotten.

In 1956 Jones's dig records were published, including a photo of the stone showing the inscription—a cross, the letters *JR*, and a human stick figure. The only comment the inscription received was a footnote, saying the markings were probably not "deliberate fakes," but were not likely made by the native users of the stone.

In 1972 a light went on in the mind of anthropologist Robert Heizer. He had first seen photos of the stone 16 years earlier when he helped prepare Jones's records for publication. Heizer wondered if the slab could be connected with the earliest European explorers of California. More specifically, he wondered if the letters *JR* referred to Juan Rodríguez Cabrillo, leader of the first Spanish expedition to reach the California coast. Cabrillo was known to most of his compatriots as Juan Rodríguez, and he died on one of the Channel Islands in early 1543. Had his shipmates scribed this stone to mark their captain's grave?

Heizer toyed with the idea and then began to investigate. Unraveling the clues provided by the inscription, he ran into the mysteries surrounding the man we call Cabrillo.

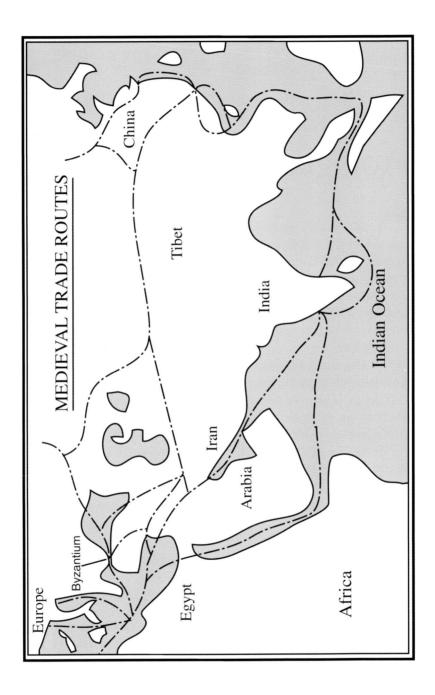

MEDIEVAL TRADE ROUTES

Europe

Byzantium

China

Tibet

India

Iran

Arabia

Egypt

Africa

Indian Ocean

1

Spice and Silk

...one pound of pepper and one pound of cinnamon, and one ounce of silk....
—entry in a medieval English record
indicating the value of a parcel of land

Juan Rodríguez Cabrillo lived during the second century of the Age of Exploration—a 400-year period (1420 to 1820) when bold Europeans undertook daring voyages and radically changed the map of the world. Cabrillo was one of these adventurers, and he added the coast of California to the known world. Few eyewitness accounts remain from the discovery voyages, and personal information about many of the explorers is sketchy. They were men of action, not letters, and much of what we know about them has to be inferred from records, which are open to interpretation.

We don't know the date and place of Cabrillo's birth. Historians guess he was born between 1498 and 1500, but they squabble over his birthplace. Many think he was Portuguese, but recently a few scholars reviewed the information and think he came from Spain (inflaming the Portuguese who proudly claim him). Uncertainty also exists about his name. What exactly was it? Until 1536, he appears in records simply as Juan Rodríguez, a name as common then as John Smith is now. Did he add Cabrillo when he became a man of means to distinguish himself from other Juan Rodríguezes? We'll never know for sure. Cabrillo's name has both Spanish and Portuguese spellings. We use the Spanish form. The Portuguese spelling—João Rodrigues Cabrilho—doesn't appear in historical records, but that doesn't mean he wasn't Portuguese. Many men from Portugal used the Spanish spelling of their names when they joined Spanish expeditions.

Whether Cabrillo was Spanish or Portuguese, we can learn a great deal about him by taking a look at the history of the Iberian Peninsula—the land that became Portugal and Spain. Cabrillo and the thousands of other Iberians who flocked to the New World were uniquely equipped by the history of their homeland for success in the New World. Centuries of warfare gave them a heritage of ironclad convictions, questing spirits, and characters tough enough not only to survive in the American wilderness, but also to conquer large portions of it.

The forging of this spirit began in the 700s when Moors (Islamic Arabs from North Africa) invaded and conquered all but a small portion of the Iberian Peninsula. Vicious warfare continued between the Christian Iberians and Islamic Moors and lasted for 800 years. When the quarrelsome Christian kingdoms that made up the Iberian Peninsula weren't fighting Moors, they fought each other. Not surprisingly, the Iberians became used to fighting, intrigue, and conquest. War became a way of life, and fighting non-Christians a holy calling. This was Cabrillo's heritage.

The Iberian Peninsula was not the Moors' only target. They also attacked the wealthy Byzantine Empire, located at the eastern end of the Mediterranean. The Byzantines asked their fellow Christians in

Europe for help. Eager to fight the followers of Islam, many European cavaliers not busy fighting Moors on their own soil set off for Byzantium in 1096, beginning what we know as the Holy Wars or Crusades. The Christians were not strong enough to defeat the Arabs in the Middle East, but their sojourn introduced them to the exotic products the Arabs obtained from the Orient. The desire for these wondrous goods changed the world.

It's hard today to imagine how important oriental spices, fabrics, and precious metals were to Europeans of the Middle Ages and Renaissance or to what lengths they would go to obtain them. Spices were the chief luxury of those times. Before refrigeration, eating fresh meat was a privilege enjoyed by few people. Most survived on dried meat that was hard as brick and frequently spoiled. Spices were all that could make it palatable. Pepper was the most valued spice, and it was imported in massive quantities. One Egyptian sultan supplied 420,000 pounds annually to Venetian traders. Monarchs exchanged gifts of pepper, and it was used in lieu of money. Cinnamon, nutmeg, and other spices were also treasured and at times took on special meaning. One record tells of an old gentleman about to be put to death giving each of his friends a nutmeg as a keepsake.

Oriental fabrics were coveted as well. The wretched woolen garments Europeans wore were heavy and itchy, and, because they were hard to wash, usually filthy and verminous. Oriental fabrics were

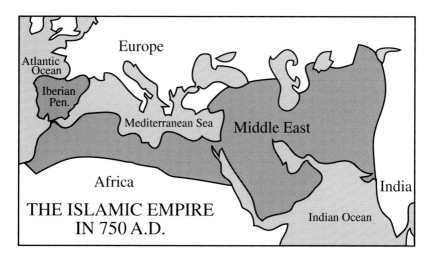

Europe

Atlantic Ocean

Iberian Pen.

Mediterranean Sea

Middle East

Africa

India

THE ISLAMIC EMPIRE IN 750 A.D.

Indian Ocean

light, flexible, and easily laundered.

The East had precious metals too. As European countries rose up out of the chaos of the Middle Ages, commerce became a way of financing growth, and metal coins were needed to carry on trade. Europe's own gold mines were exhausted, and German silver mines could not keep up with the demand. So the Orient was the source not only of luxuries, but also the means of economic expansion.

Very few Europeans had seen the Orient or the Indies, as Japan, China, the Ryukyus, Spice Islands, Indonesia, Thailand, and all else between them and India were known. And their location relative to Europe was also a mystery to the average European. A few, like Marco Polo, made it there and back in the 13th and 14th centuries, fueling the imagination of Europe's inhabitants with fantastic tales. They reported that in the mysterious lands of Cipango (Japan), Cathay, India, and the thousands of islands of the Malay archipelago, were such amazing sights as dancing horses, white elephants, and the footprint of Adam, said to be 11 spans (about 99 inches) long.

Commodities from the East were available to Europe but at a high price. The trade routes were firmly controlled by middlemen, including the hated Arabs, who charged outrageous fees for their services. Some merchants and adventurers contemplated bypassing the Arabs by seeking a direct route to the Indies, but this was a mind-boggling task for medieval people. An educated few thought the world was round and conjectured the Orient could be reached by sailing west. However, the distance from Europe to China was unknown, and the waters between the two continents were thought to be fraught with monsters and whirlpools, not to mention the challenge of sailing up the

slope of the earth's curved surface.

Even if one could cope with these problems, navigational methods were so primitive it was impossible to ensure finding the way home if one reached the East in the first place. Time and resources were needed to develop better means of navigation, but they were eaten up by war.

Of Cabrillo's two probable homelands, Portugal had a head start in exploration. The Moors were driven out of Portugal in 1143, nearly 350 years before Spain was free of them. With the Moors gone, Portugal focused on trade and exploration. Portuguese merchant seamen inched out along the Atlantic coast to trade, but without adequate means of navigation, they couldn't undertake major voyages.

Prince Henry of Portugal, who became known as Henry the Navigator, changed this situation in 1470 by founding a school of navigation, which was also a clearinghouse for maritime knowledge. Appropriately enough, it was located "where land endeth and where beginneth sea" on an austere point called Sagres on the coast of Portugal. There, knowledge from an international group of navigators, mathematicians, astronomers, and cartographers was pooled and led to improvements in ship design, charts, and navigational instruments and techniques.

On the practical side, almost yearly, expeditions from the school sailed farther and farther south down the coast of Africa. Their primary goal was to find a route to the eastern border of the Moslem nations. Prince Henry, like most of his Christian contemporaries, wanted to continue fighting the Moors on their homeland. A route to the Indies would also be nice.

Sea monsters lurked in the waters
of 16th-century maps, reminding
mariners of the perils awaiting
them in the deep.

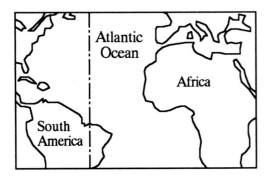

Map showing the demarcation line of the 1494 Treaty of Tordesilla. Unexplored areas east of the line belonged to Portugal. Those west of the line belonged to Spain.

Lessons learned from each journey were added to the theoretical knowledge developed at the school and then used during successive voyages. The navigators who made the boldest discoveries were well rewarded by Prince Henry and his successors. This was the first time in Europe that maritime knowledge was systematically collected and compiled, and goals consistently sought. In 1503, a major goal was achieved when a Portuguese-trained expedition circumnavigated Africa and reached India, establishing a trade route to the beginning of the mysterious East. Over time, the Portuguese established and maintained permanent colonies at the Madeira and Cape Verde islands, Portuguese Guinea, Angola, Goa, and Mozambique, assuring their sovereignty over the route.

While Portugal was free to take advantage of the improvements in marine science, Spain was still bogged down fighting Moors. Finally, in 1492, Granada, the last toehold of the Moors on the Iberian Peninsula, surrendered. Spanish monarchs Ferdinand and Isabella had united the other kingdoms of Spain into one powerful country and were now ready to compete with Portugal in finding a trade route to the Orient.

Because Portugal had obtained from the pope exclusive rights to "regions lying southward and eastward" from Portugal, on the grounds that it was doing crusading work for the Church, only north and west remained for Ferdinand and Isabella to explore. With the help of Christopher Columbus, Spain went west and discovered the American continents. In turn, Spain received from the pope rights to all lands west of an arbitrary line 100 leagues (roughly 318 nautical miles) west of the Azores. Portugal was unhappy with this disposition. After some wrangling, the two countries signed the Treaty of Tordesilla in 1494, which moved the line of demarcation about 270 leagues west, unknowingly entitling Portugal to the northeast corner of South America.

After completing four voyages to the New World, Columbus went to his grave in 1506 believing he had reached the Indies. But by the time of his death, enough people had seen the real Indies to know that whatever Columbus had found wasn't the Indies. At first the Spanish were irritated by this additional obstacle between them and the East, but soon they realized it might offer riches of its own. Explorers would continue to seek a route to the Indies, but on the way they would look for treasure. Juan Rodríguez Cabrillo would be fortunate to be in on some of the richest discoveries.

2

The *Hidalgos*

We came to serve God and also get rich.
— Bernal Díaz del Castillo, conquistador

In 1552, the wife of Juan Rodríguez Cabrillo testified that her husband "came to these Indies more than forty years ago." Some historians think young Cabrillo, known then as Juan Rodríguez, arrived as early as 1510. Historian Harry Kelsey (who believes Cabrillo was Spanish) speculates Cabrillo may have been an orphan taken into the household of a Spanish merchant and then sent to the Americas on a trading voyage. Diego Sánchez de Ortega, a close friend of Cabrillo, was the son of such a merchant in Seville. Perhaps they came across the Atlantic together.

Whenever and however Cabrillo came to the New World, he joined a stream of Spanish adventurers who became his teachers, mentors, and companions. Many were *hidalgos*, Spanish noblemen required to be available at a moment's notice to serve the crown. *Hidalgos* kept weapons, horses, and servants for this purpose and weren't allowed to do manual labor. Although they were dedicated to the king and queen, Spain had such an overabundance of these noblemen that the royal court couldn't support them all, and many were poor. Poverty grated heavily on these knights who, besides being brave, were intensely (and sometimes ludicrously) proud. As long as they were involved in honorable activities like fighting infidels, they were happy, but when the Moors were driven out of Spain at the end of the 15th century, the *hidalgos* had little to do and grew restless. The discovery of the New World gave them an opportunity to again find

honor serving God and country and perhaps get rich as well.

The cavaliers who went to the New World and took part in the Spanish conquest became known as conquistadors, or conquerors. Historian Albert Man describes them as "experienced soldiers...[with] an inner strength born of confidence in the righteousness of their cause. Conquistadors believed that what they did was right." Deep and unquestioning religious faith was the source of their belief, and they wore it like armor against non-Christians. Combining this ironclad faith with a background of growing up seeing soldiers return from war with Islamic heads tied to their saddles, the Spaniards were well equipped to carry out the brutal tasks of conquest. Young Cabrillo was trained by Old World crusaders like these, and he too became a conquistador and *hidalgo*.

Cabrillo's first commander was the *hidalgo* Pánfilo de Narváez, whom Gonzalo Fernández de Oviedo y Valdez, the official Spanish historian of the Indies, described as having come to the New World "with only a sword and a shield, searching for adventure." He was also reputed to be a good horseman and courageous soldier, but a mean, selfish, and not overly bright leader. Cabrillo's service with him may have started as early as 1511.

At that time, Narváez and Diego Velázquez, a successful soldier and wealthy New World landowner, were sent to explore Cuba. A small gold mine had been found on the island of Hispaniola, the first Spanish settlement in the New World. Narváez and Velázquez were to search Cuba for gold and conquer its natives. The army they led consisted of 30 crossbowmen, 300 soldiers, and the many pages, aides, and native slaves that commonly made up the retinue of Spanish armies. Cabrillo may have been in this force.

The conquest of Cuba was bloody; in fact, it was so needlessly bloody that the expedition's chaplain, Bartolomé de las Casas, quit in outrage. "I saw such terrible cruelties done there," he wrote, "as I had never seen before nor thought to see." The Arawak Indians of Cuba were peaceful and friendly and thought the strange-looking white men were immortals from the heavens. Thousands of these passive natives were murdered without provocation. Las Casas told of one incident when Narváez's men hacked to death a village of Arawaks who had docilely greeted the Spaniards and fed them dinner. The soldiers enjoyed the meal and then turned on the villagers, killing them all. The Arawaks eventually realized the Spaniards were merely mortal and fought back. But their clubs were no match for Spanish cannons and crossbows.

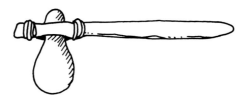

Those Indians that weren't killed during the conquest of Cuba and who didn't die of smallpox brought by Narváez's men, were enslaved in the *encomienda* system. As rewards for service to the crown, high-ranking personnel were given Indian villages as *encomiendas*. In theory, the villagers were to provide goods and services to their Spanish landlords, and the landlords were to provide religious education and protection for the villagers. In practice, the Spanish frequently worked the native men to death mining gold, while the women and children died of starvation with no men to help them work their fields.

Las Casas and other priests complained to the Spanish monarch about the atrocious treatment of the natives, and King Charles I,

Ferdinand and Isabella's grandson (who became Holy Roman Emperor Charles V in 1519), sent out a commission of friars to evaluate the situation. Although Spain had never approved of slavery, the friars saw that the Indians were essential to mining and would not work without being forced. In this situation, the good fathers justified slavery as the only way the natives could be kept in contact with the whites, learn about God, and be converted. The friars recommended many measures to protect the natives, and the king backed them up with laws limiting and controlling slavery. But, although the power of Spain's monarchy usually reached across the Atlantic, in this case it didn't. "*Obedézcase, pero no se cumpla*" (let it be obeyed, but not enforced) was the attitude of Spanish colonists about this and other rulings that didn't match their interests. The mines in Cuba were rich. The majority of the Arawaks of the Greater Antilles were dead within 30 years. Blacks from Africa were imported to replace them.

(Some historians believe the slaughter of the Arawaks didn't go unrevenged. Syphilis first appeared in Europe in a few Spanish ports soon after Columbus returned from the New World. Historians conjecture his sailors got the deadly spirochete from the Arawaks among whom the disease was common and not virulent.)

After Cuba was secured, Velázquez became governor. With promises of land to farm and slaves to farm it, he attracted many *hidalgos* to the island. Cuba prospered with a new colonial aristocracy supported by slaves who raised sugar, tobacco, and cacao, and mined gold. Velázquez, however, was not satisfied. Greedy and restless, he chafed with ambition to expand his wealth through further explora-

From left to right, Diego Velázquez, Charles V of Spain, and Father Bartolomé de las Casas.

tion. In 1515, he sailed to Spain seeking royal permission for colonists to build their own ships and trade among the islands.

Up to that time, the king had tightly controlled all exploration, trade, and colonization in the New World. Anyone wishing to undertake an expedition had had to seek his permission. However, in 1516, the crown approved Velázquez's request, and although individuals had to give a fifth of their profits to the king, they now had more freedom and incentive to explore and seek treasure. The business of exploration boomed. And as the potential for profits grew, jealousy, rivalry, and intrigue broke out among the explorers. Who would find treasure first? Who would get the largest share?

Two small expeditions from Cuba, one outfitted by Velázquez, brought back small gold ornaments and jewels from the Yucatán peninsula of Mexico. Members of the expeditions had seen huge stone temples that hinted at the riches to be found on the mainland. The natives who built them were Mayans, people whose once highly developed civilization was in decline, but the remaining Mayans told of a fabulously wealthy and powerful civilization inland. Called Mexico, it was ruled by the Aztecs—people so powerful, the Mayans trembled when they mentioned them.

When Velázquez heard of Mexico, he brushed aside the Mayans' warning, and, according to historian William H. Prescott, "The heart of the governor swelled with rapture as he saw his dreams of avarice and ambition so likely to be realized." Velázquez quickly packaged the king's share of the gold and sent it with his chaplain to Spain to get the king's permission to conquer Mexico. But, in 1518, without waiting for the king's response, he began assembling an armada. Other people were showing interest in Mexico, and Velázquez wanted the wealth of the Aztecs for himself. To command the expedition, he chose his secretary, Hernán Cortés, an equally ambitious and restless Spaniard.

Where was Cabrillo while Velázquez was plotting and planning? Some of his companions reported that by 1520 Cabrillo was a skilled soldier and seaman who knew about building ships. From their comments, we can assume fairly safely that between his arrival in Cuba and 1520, Cabrillo continued to be trained to fight Indians by Narváez and men like him. He may also have gone on one of the Yucatán expeditions. If so, he would have gained experience in both seamanship and soldiering.

Because of the king's ruling that individuals could build their own ships to explore and trade, shipbuilding and outfitting grew in the New World. Havana was known then as Puerto de Carenas—the place where ships are careened. Careening entailed hauling a ship out of water to recaulk its hull. Materials for this process and other repairs, and shipwrights capable to do the work, were available in the New World by at least 1518, so Cabrillo may well have learned about ship repair and construction in Puerto de Carenas.

Although we can't be sure how and where he gained his training, by 1520 Cabrillo was described by fellow conquistador Francisco López as able to "carry out orders both as a soldier and as one charged with preparing material and fittings for [boats].... This Juan Rodríguez was a man of the sea, and he understood that sort of work."

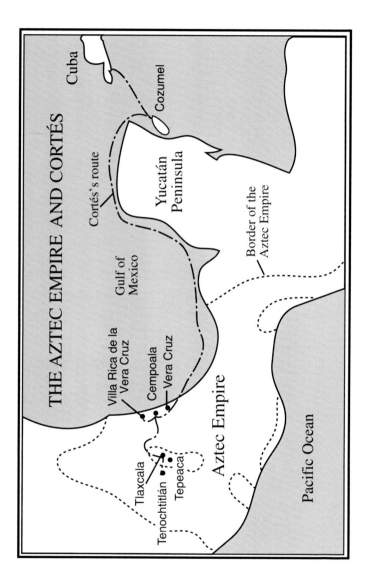

THE AZTEC EMPIRE AND CORTÉS

Cuba

Cozumel

Cortés's route

Yucatán
Peninsula

Gulf of
Mexico

Border of the
Aztec Empire

Villa Rica de la
Vera Cruz

Cempoala
Vera Cruz

Aztec Empire

Tlaxcala

Tenochtitlán

Tepeaca

Pacific Ocean

3

The Classic Conquistador

We Spanish suffer from a disease of the heart which can only be cured by gold.

—Hernán Cortés

While Cabrillo was a man of practical skills, Hernán Cortés, who would lead Velázquez's expedition to Mexico, was a person of far-reaching talents and dazzling charm. He was the quintessential conquistador and classic New World adventurer of Cabrillo's time. Unlike Cabrillo, much is known about this fascinating rascal, whose tactical brilliance and sheer audacity made him one of history's giants.

Cortés arrived in the New World in 1504 at the age of 21. When the governor of Hispaniola offered him land to farm, Cortés replied, "I came to get gold, not till the soil like a peasant," but he accepted the offer. Diego Velázquez, who was then a landowner and lieutenant to the Hispaniola governor, became Cortés's mentor, teaching him, among other things, to fight Indians—an activity much to Cortés's liking. When Velázquez became governor of Cuba, he took Cortés with him as his secretary and field representative, and made him rich with *encomiendas*. Cortés's wit, bravery, and polished charm made him popular with both aristocrats and common people alike. When Velázquez needed someone to lead his Mexico expedition, he chose Cortés, despite growing concern about the ambitious younger man's loyalty.

This was the chance Cortés had been waiting for. Using his own money, he recruited soldiers and outfitted an 11-ship fleet, which carried 508 soldiers, 100 sailors, several hundred Indians, 10 large cannons, 4 small field guns, and 16 horses. In early 1519 this small army first touched land on Cozumel, an island off the Yucatán peninsula, and then they sailed west and south along the peninsula's coast toward the Aztec empire. Along the way, they established a reputation for invincibility among the natives they encountered.

The conquistadors were excellent fighters, but even before they drew their swords, they had a psychological advantage over the natives. Most had never seen white men or horses before and thought both were gods. Cortés slashed his way through hostile tribes with no more concern for them than Narváez had shown in Cuba. But he was wise enough to make allies of the friendly natives and even invited those he defeated to join him. His requests paid off—many natives joined the Spaniards out of admiration for their valor and hatred for the Aztecs.

The Aztecs had not always been so powerful. Two hundred years earlier they had been a small band of nomads, serving as mercenary soldiers for various tribes while they sought a homeland promised by their gods. They were a fiercely independent people with a martial way of life. The tribes who employed them valued their services, but were often so frightened by them they didn't retain them for long.

The glyph for conquest was one of the most frequently used symbols in the writings of the Aztecs. In this example, it is combined with "old man," the glyph for one of the towns conquered by the Aztecs.

In 1325 on an island in Lake Texcoco in the Mexican Highlands, the Aztecs saw the omen an oracle had predicted would indicate their homeland—an eagle with a snake in its talons, perched on a cactus growing out of a rock—and there they built their capital. From this base they swept through Mexico, conquering most of the tribes they met. By the time Cortés arrived, their empire reached from the Atlantic to the Pacific oceans and included nearly 80,000 square miles and 15 million people.

The Aztecs allowed the tribes they conquered to function indepen-

Aztec priests gouged open the chests of their victims and removed the still-beating heart. This mosaic-handled obsidian sacrificial knife is thought to have been given to Cortés by Montezuma.

dently as long as they paid heavy taxes and provided whatever services the Aztecs required. Frequently this included helping them put down rebelling tribes, for the conquered tribes chafed heavily under the Aztec yoke.

Secure and wealthy, the Aztecs created a sophisticated culture governed by a rigid power hierarchy. At the top was an absolute monarch who traditionally was trained as a military leader. When Cortés arrived, Montezuma II, was in power. Both a soldier and a priest, Montezuma began his rule as an exemplary military general, but as time passed, he became increasingly superstitious and self-absorbed. He let his captains lead the army, while he spent his time trying to soothe the implacable Aztec gods.

While the Spaniards felt supported and sustained by their religion, the Aztecs were in a constant struggle with theirs. Prescott reports that in 1486, more than 70,000 people were sacrificed at the opening of a temple to Huitzilopotchli, the gruesome god of war, whom the Aztecs believed required human sacrifice to keep the world in order. Although that was an extreme occasion, human sacrifice was a daily occurrence. Wars were fought to capture prisoners for the sacrificial altars, which were kept busy daily, dispatching enough unfortunate souls to keep the sun rising.

When Montezuma heard of the Spaniards' arrival, he was terrified. Aztec legend predicted that in the year 1519, the same year Cortés

Unlike many of the Aztec gods, Quetzalcoátl was adamantly against human sacrifice. Here, he takes a prisoner, undoubtedly a practitioner of that bloody rite.

arrived, the Aztec god of wisdom would come from across the Atlantic and destroy the practitioners of human sacrifice. This god, known as Quetzalcóatl, was white-skinned and wore a beard and was expected to take over the throne of Mexico. Montezuma was sure Cortés was Quetzalcóatl. When he received word that Cortés wished to visit him, he sent polite greetings but asked the Spaniard to return to wherever he came from. Unfortunately for the Aztecs, Montezuma accompanied his message with fabulous gifts—a gold helmet filled with gold dust, discs the size of cartwheels of solid gold and silver, and many other treasures—which only increased Cortés's commitment to make the Aztec empire his own.

Montezuma never sent the full force of the Aztec empire against the Spaniards, but he did order some of his tribes to stop their progress as they proceeded toward the Aztec capital. Cortés, however, was aware of the unrest among the tribes and employed his gifts of persuasion and Machiavellian cunning to manipulate them in his favor. In dealings like this he was immeasurably helped by a young native woman named Doña Marina.

Doña Marina was a chief's daughter who had been sold into slavery by her mother. Soon after the Spaniards arrived in Mexico, she was given to them, along with 19 other female slaves, as a peace offering by the Tabascan tribe. Prescott describes her as being "in the morning of life" and possessed of "uncommon personal attractions." She spoke both Mayan and Aztec and quickly learned Spanish. When Cortés realized her skill with languages, she became his main interpreter as well as his private secretary and mistress. (She bore him a son, and was eventually given in marriage to one of the conquistadors.) Besides interpreting for Cortés, Marina taught him about the ways and beliefs of the natives of Mexico, which assisted him in developing strategies to deal with them.

Not all the natives were easily subdued, and some horrendous battles occurred with the Spanish facing what appeared to be impossible odds. A campaign against the warriors of Tlaxcala reportedly pitted 500 Spanish soldiers, supported by 2,500 Indian allies, against a Tlaxcalan force estimated to be between 30,000 and 150,000 warriors. (Eyewitness estimates of army sizes throughout the conquest of Mexico disagree frustratingly.) In five tumultuous battles, each Spaniard was wounded and many were killed, but the conquistadors still managed to overwhelm the Indians. Their disciplined tactics and superior weapons tipped the scale in their favor, as did the Indians' practice of taking prisoners for human sacrifice. While the Spaniards could shoot and slash to kill, the Indians tried to wound their enemies so they could have victims for the sacrificial altar.

The conquistadors ultimately defeated the Tlaxcalans, but the Tlaxcalans were so impressed with the Spaniards' courage and military prowess, they joined forces and remained invaluable allies throughout the conquests of Mexico and Central America.

In this illustration adapted from an Aztec drawing, Doña Marina interprets for Cortés and Montezuma.

The troops of Cortés felt the strain of such battles, and some of them still felt loyal to Governor Velázquez. Cortés had made it clear, however, that he no longer felt any allegiance to his old boss, and he had gone so far as to petition the king for sole right to explore and conquer Mexico. Cortés claimed his men had begged him to do this or he would have remained loyal to his old benefactor. But in fact, after he established the town of Villa Rica de la Vera Cruz (Rich Town of the True Cross) on the Mexican coast, he had his cronies persuade the rest of his men to elect him mayor, which gave him a legitimate position from which to act independently. When some of the soldiers threatened to desert because of Cortés's actions, Cortés cut off their escape route—and his own way home to safety—by sinking all but one of his ships. Trapped on the Mexican mainland, his men worked together and fought valiantly.

In this single-minded manner, Cortés battled and maneuvered his way around discontented troops and hostile tribes and into the Aztec capital where Montezuma surrendered without a fight, defeated by his superstitions. His chieftains were outraged, but their habit of obedience to their monarch was strong, and they stood by helplessly as Montezuma handed the reins of the empire to Cortés.

Back in Cuba, Velázquez was furious when he learned Cortés was trying to cut him out of the Mexican profits. Livid with "disappointed avarice," as Prescott puts it, he prepared another fleet to capture the traitorous Cortés. At first, the governor planned to lead it himself, but after realizing his vast bulk (he was grossly fat) was unsuited for the rigors of the journey, he appointed Cabrillo's commander, Panfilo de Narváez, as expedition leader. Narváez had successfully conquered Cuba, and Velázquez hoped he would do just as well against Cortés. In March 1520, the fleet's 19 ships set sail for Mexico carrying 1,400 soldiers, 90 crossbowmen, 80 horsemen, 70 arquebusiers, 2 master gunners, and 20 cannons. Among the crossbowmen was Juan Rodríguez Cabrillo.

This army, like that of Cortés, was well-equipped with a variety of arms and soldiers skilled in their use. By becoming a crossbowman, Cabrillo had taken one of the few ways a common man could move up in the world, for crossbowmen and arquebusiers were among the elite of the military. Crossbows required strength, skill, and patience to fire.

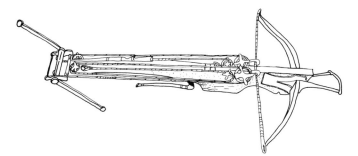

Made of wood and steel, they had enough force to pierce armor. Depending on their size, they were cocked by devices with varying cranking power. Small ones required a ratchet device, called a cranequin, which needed only one hand to turn, while large military crossbows, like the ones used by Cabrillo, required a windlass and both hands.

To cock his crossbow, a soldier stood with one foot in the bow's stirrup, attached the cranking device to the end of the stock, and then cranked the string back and hooked it over a lock. Next, he removed the windlass or cranequin with a few reverse turns and returned it to a hook on his belt. Finally, he placed a bolt (a short arrow, also called a quarrel) in place, aimed, and pulled the trigger. All these maneuvers took time and left the crossbowman vulnerable. In open combat, a shield propped in front of him or held by a servant gave protection. A good crossbowman could fire once a minute.

The conquistadors used a variety of other weapons. The standard was a broad sword, which was swung to cut a great swath in front of the user. Made of steel, the broad sword usually was engraved with an inspiring motto. One sword left by a member of Coronado's expedition in the mid-1500s in what is now Kansas says, "Never draw me without motive, never sheathe me without honor." Other weapons included small swords, daggers, pikes, lances, cannons, and arquebuses.

Cannons were individually cast, giving each unique characteristics. Soldiers gave them names like whistler, bouncer, and screamer to describe their quirks in firing. Cannons either had small wheels or were carried in carts. The first handguns, which appeared in the late 1300s, were actually just miniature cannons. The arquebus was a larger and improved version of the handgun, with a touch hole on the

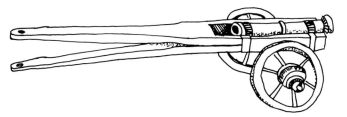

side and a flashpan next to it that held powder. It was fired by touching a burning fuse to the powder. A wooden handle like a pistol's projected down from the arquebus's barrel, and the barrel's forward end was steadied with a forked stick during firing.

The uniforms worn by the armies of Cortés and Narváez were not standardized. Soldiers wore what they had, and their attire varied depending on their rank and personal wealth. Crossbowmen like Cabrillo wore a helmet with a narrow brim or no brim at all, to avoid interference with firing. Metal breastplates were good protection but constrained movement, so brigandines were preferred. Brigandines were vests made of an outer layer of leather and an inner layer of canvas with a layer of small, square, steel plates riveted in between. Under this, a soldier might wear a chainmail shirt, and complete his attire with metal knee guards, a chainmail neck protector, and metal "lobster tails" to protect his upper legs. The brigandine alone could weigh 35 pounds. Marching in this array, particularly in the tropical heat of parts of Mexico, was exhausting. Not surprisingly, the conquistadors eventually adopted the thickly quilted cotton armor worn by American natives.

The conquistadors wore their armor day and night during the conquest of Mexico. Cabrillo and his companions must have suffered mightily from the heat during their first days there. Narváez may have been successful in Cuba, but in other efforts, as writer Evan Connell puts it, he was "one of history's classic bunglers." He chose to camp and establish a colony on the scorched sand dunes where the modern city of Vera Cruz now stands. Besides being hot, this blighted spot was, according to 19th-century historian Prescott, "surrounded by stagnant marshes, the exhalations from which quickened by the heat into the pestilent malaria."

Fortunately for the soldiers, Narváez abandoned his notion of a colony and moved his troops north to Cempoalla, a large Indian city, or pueblo, near Villa Rica de la Vera Cruz. As the soldiers marched along, Cabrillo and his companions watched the landscape change from barren waste to lush tropical plains and forests laced with streams and rivers. Brilliantly colored parrots winged through air heavy with exotic scents, and flowering vines cascaded from immense trees. Even the conquistadors, who weren't overly blessed with sensitivity, were touched by the elegance of this landscape.

Other sights chilled them. Mutilated human bodies and carefully stacked human skulls (one conquistador claimed to have counted 100,000 skulls in one location) repulsed the Spaniards and gave evidence of the scale of human sacrifice in Mexico. Indications of these ghastly practices would become common sights to Cabrillo and his fellows and reinforce their belief in the inherent superiority of Christians over idolators.

Despite their barbaric religious practices, the Totonac Indians of Cempoalla, like the Aztecs and many other Mexican tribes, were cultured, handsome, and wealthy. Between 20,000 and 30,000 people lived in Cempoalla. They loved flowers and greeted the Spaniards with colorful garlands. The white stucco walls of their impeccably clean city reflected the sun so brightly that at first the Spaniards thought the walls were silver. Cempoalla became Narváez's headquarters. From there he arrogantly announced his intentions to capture and hang Cortés.

This pronouncement quickly traveled the 200 miles to Tenochtitlán, the Aztec capital, via the well-organized Aztec grapevine of couriers. Trained to run swiftly from early childhood, the couriers worked in

relays and passed messages from one to another along well-developed routes. The messages were written in the Aztecs' sophisticated hieroglyphics, which were capable of conveying complex meaning. Paintings sometimes supplemented them. (Paintings of Cortés's ships, men, and horses accompanied the message that informed Montezuma of the Spaniards' arrival in Mexico.) The couriers of the Aztec system were so fast and well organized that messages could travel between 100 and 200 miles a day.

In Tenochtitlán, Montezuma was delighted to hear of Narváez's intentions. Although he was still too intimidated to act directly against Cortés, he was eager to be rid of him, and sent gifts to the newly arrived Spaniards suggesting they work together to destroy Cortés.

Cortés heard of this scheme and knew he'd be lost if the Aztecs allied with Narváez. After learning of Narváez's location, he left Tenochtitlán in charge of his second-in-command, Pedro de Alvarado (who would later become Cabrillo's commander), and marched with about 300 soldiers to Cempoalla. Boldly, they attacked Narváez's much larger force in the middle of a rainy night and quickly defeated them. Narváez's inexperienced troops were no match for the battle-hardened soldiers of Cortés. Cortés jailed Narváez, who had lost an eye in the battle. Then, with typical aplomb and expediency, he convinced Narváez's army to join him.

Recruiting the leaderless troops was not difficult. Narváez's personality had not inspired loyalty. Besides being a bungler, he was described by Connell as "a most unpleasant personage even among odious companions...." Because most of his men had only come to Mexico, or New Spain as it was soon called, to find gold, it was easy for them to transfer their allegiance to Cortés who promised to share his profits with them.

We don't know what role Cabrillo played in that night of fighting. Evidence indicates he may have been among those in Narváez's force who were already sympathetic to Cortés, having known him in Cuba. Before Cortés attacked Narváez, he secretly contacted these people and promised them rewards for not fighting him. So Cabrillo may have played a passive role in his first battle in New Spain. Soon afterward, he was given the honor of commanding a *cuadrilla*, or squad, of crossbowmen in the army of Cortés.

While Cortés was rejoicing about the additions to his force, a desperate message arrived from Pedro de Alvarado. The Aztecs were attacking the Spanish encampment. If Cortés wished to keep the Aztec empire, he had better return quickly to Tenochtitlán. Cortés, worried that his new recruits might balk at facing the mighty Aztecs, assembled them and addressed them in inspiring terms few could resist. He called upon their honor and faith, and beseeched them to serve God and country and follow him to glory against the heathenish Aztecs. Then, writes Bernal Díaz del Castillo, a member of Cortés's army and one of the few eyewitness chroniclers of the conquest of Mexico, "one and all offered themselves to him to go with us, [but] if they had known the power of Mexico, it is certain that not one of them would have gone."

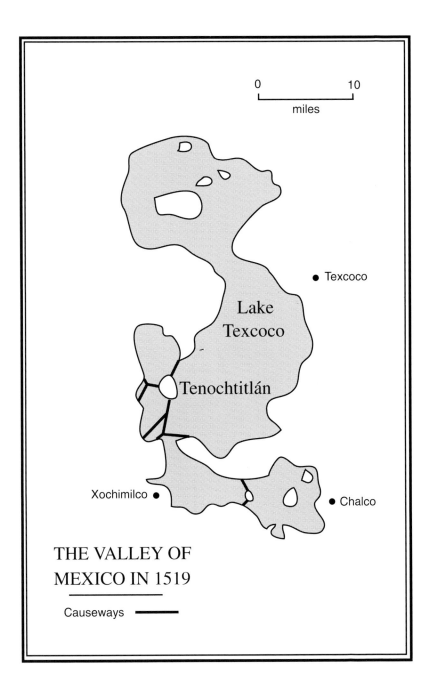

0   10
miles

● Texcoco

Lake
Texcoco

Tenochtitlán

Xochimilco ●

● Chalco

THE VALLEY OF
MEXICO IN 1519

Causeways ━━━

4

The Enchanted City

I do not know how to tell of the great squadrons of warriors who came to attack us that day....
— Bernal Díaz del Castillo, conquistador

By forced march, the army of Cortés with its new members traveled 200 miles through foothills and mountains, up to the Valley of Mexico in the Mexican Highlands. There, at an elevation of 7,244 feet, Lake Texcoco stretched before them surrounded by mountains. From the surface of the 400-square-mile lake rose the gleaming city of Tenochtitlán.

The city had been founded on two small islands which the Aztecs expanded with floating gardens. Over time, the gardens rooted in the bottom of the shallow lake, and buildings were built upon them. Canals wove through the spotlessly clean city, and flower gardens and orchards flourished. A zoo and aviaries entertained the royalty, whose palaces were in the middle of the city. Above all rose the stone pyramids of the Aztec gods. Broad causeways connected the capital to the edge of the lake where other magnificent cities stood. With more than 300,000 people, Tenochtitlán was larger than any European capital of that time.

No records tell us what Cabrillo thought when he first glimpsed the heart of the Aztec empire, but he probably was as overwhelmed as the members of Cortés's original army had been when they arrived eight months earlier. Díaz had a hard time finding words to express the magnitude of that experience. "I do not know how to describe it," he wrote, "seeing things as we did that had never been heard or seen before, not even dreamed about."

In those days, many young men had been encouraged to seek their fortunes in the New World by chivalrous stories and romantic novels that were popular at that time. Written as authentic accounts, they told of the exploits of cavaliers in strange and wonderful lands. Fictional stories like these circulated with reports of true adventures, like those of Marco Polo, confusing readers about what was fact and what was fantasy.

Tenochtitlán reminded Díaz of the enchanted cities described in one such book. Other soldiers were so astounded by the cities, they thought they were dreaming. The causeways on that day were thronged with richly dressed natives, conducting business and attending markets full of exotic food and wares. The mighty Montezuma himself had come to greet them, arriving on a gold and silver litter. When he alighted, servants shaded him with a canopy of green feathers embroidered with pearls and gold, and wherever he walked, more servants ran before him covering the ground with cloths so his gold-soled sandals never touched the earth.

The unworldly conquistadors thought they had entered the Arabian nights and eagerly marched into the city.

Although the causeway was suspiciously empty eight months later, on June 24, 1520, when Cortés returned to Tenochtitlán with Narváez's troops, the soldiers entered the city just as eagerly. The Aztecs might pose a hideous threat, but their capital mesmerized the Spaniards. Besides gold, it offered them adventure and romance—a chance to become like the heroes in the tales they admired. In reality, soldiers like Cabrillo could not hope to become rich from conquest like their leaders. But they could achieve glory, and that was enough to keep them following Cortés. A half century later, Díaz grandly recalled reentering Tenochtitlán. "What men," he wrote, "have there been in the world who have shown such daring?"

Inside the city, Cortés marched his reinforcements to the fine stone palace where previously he and his men had lived in luxury as the conquerors of the Aztec empire. Now all that awaited them were hungry and anxious Spaniards. The Aztecs had ended their siege but refused to bring the Spaniards food. On questioning, it became clear that Alvarado, who had been left in charge of the camp, had provoked the Aztec attack. After giving permission for a festival, he and his men killed the participants—hundreds of unarmed nobles—and plundered the bodies of their gold ornaments. Cortés was furious with Alvarado, but he was sure Montezuma could calm the angry natives as he had done many times before for him.

This time he was wrong. Superstition and fear may have cowed Montezuma, but his people weren't so easily daunted. They realized the Spaniards weren't gods, and despite their loyalty to Montezuma, there was only so much they could take. The Spaniards had emptied their treasure houses, desecrated their gods, and emasculated their leader. After Alvarado's massacre, their pent-up fury exploded. When Cortés sent Montezuma to soothe them, they stoned and killed their emperor. Then, rallying around Montezuma's brother and later his nephew, the Aztecs attacked the Spaniards.

This was the first time that Cabrillo and the other soldiers of Narváez had faced Mexican Indians in battle. Just the sight of these savage warriors in their brilliantly colored battle attire was enough to daunt the bravest newcomer. Historian Prescott describes them:

> The common file wore no covering except a girdle round the loins. Their bodies were painted with the appropriate colors of the chieftain whose banner they followed....The caciques and principal warriors were clothed in a quilted tunic, two inches thick, which, fitting close to the body, protected, also, the thighs and the shoulders. Over this the wealthier Indians wore cuirasses of thin gold plate, or silver. Their legs were defended by leathern boots or sandals, trimmed with gold. But the most brilliant part of their costume was a rich mantle of the

plumaje or feather-work, embroidered with curious art....
This graceful and picturesque dress was surmounted by a
fantastic head-piece made of wood or leather, representing
the head of some wild animal, and frequently displaying a
formidable array of teeth...producing a most grotesque and
hideous effect.

Light but strong wicker shields protected the Indians from all but
a well-placed crossbow shot. With deadly accuracy, the Aztecs used
slings, bows and stone-tipped arrows, and spears with copper or stone
heads. They threw javelins with incredible force from throwing sticks,
called *atlatls*, and they could easily decapitate a man with their form
of broad sword, called a *macana* or *maquahuitl*. Three or four feet
long, these swords were made of wood several inches wide with a
groove cut around the edge. From the groove, projected razor-sharp
pieces of obsidian.

Armed with these weapons, tens of thousands of Aztecs stormed
the Spaniards' quarters pelting the conquistadors with stones, arrows,
and spears. Several times the Spaniards broke out of the besieged
palace and charged the Indians on horseback, but the Aztecs pushed
them back. Although the Spaniards' weapons were superior, the sheer
number, tenacity, and frenzied valor of the Aztecs were unbeatable. As
Díaz writes, "...neither cannon nor muskets nor crossbows availed, nor
hand-to-hand fighting, nor killing thirty or forty of them every time we
charged, for they still fought on in as close ranks and with more energy
than in the beginning."

Realizing they had to escape from the city, Cortés had a portable
bridge built. The Aztecs had cut gaps in the causeways leading out of
Tenochtitlán, and the bridge was needed to fill them. Cortés planned
for it to be moved from gap to gap as the Spaniards escaped. At
midnight during a rainstorm on July 10—a night now known as *La
Noche Triste*, or night of sadness—the conquistadors and their Tlaxcalan
allies began to leave the city. Burdened by baggage and with no place
to hide on the open causeways, many were easy marks for the Aztecs
who attacked from canoes. The portable bridge, under the care of
Alvarado and the crossbowmen, had to be abandoned when it became
clogged with bodies.

This young warrior wears an eagle helmet and the standard of his chieftain attached to a wooden frame on his back.

The retreat lasted five days until the Spaniards reached the territory of friendly Indians. By that time they had lost all their artillery and most of their weapons. Human casualties were also high with the heaviest occurring among Narváez's men who had loaded themselves down with gold and then drowned in the lake. Cabrillo escaped that fate. He may have been one of several hundred crossbowmen with Alvarado and the portable bridge. Only five of that group survived. Wherever he was, Cabrillo was lucky to escape. Out of the roughly 1,500 Spaniards and 2,000 Tlaxcalans that were in the city, more than 900 Spaniards and 1,000 Tlaxcalans were killed or captured and sacrificed to the Aztec gods.

*A horse has fallen off the causeway during the Spaniards' escape
from Tenochtitlán.*

One would think after such casualties, the conquistadors would
have returned to the islands, but the indomitable band regrouped and
planned their return to Tenochtitlán. With trickery and bribery, they
acquired new soldiers and weapons from ships just arriving in New
Spain. But the key to their return would be 13 small ships called
bergantines that Cortés ordered built. With them, the conquistadors
could overcome the Aztecs' advantage on the causeways. Cabrillo
played a major role in their construction, and from this point onward,
details of his life become more available.

Before Cortés sank his original fleet, he had the iron fittings,
anchors, cables, rigging, and sails removed. A thousand Indian slaves
(acquired from raids on pueblos sympathetic to the Aztecs) now
carried these supplies from Villa Rica de la Vera Cruz to Tepeaca, the
Spaniards' new base. Thousands more cut timber for the ships.
Cabrillo's job was to produce the pitch-and-tallow sealing material
used to protect the hulls from sea worms. With a working party of
natives, he extracted pitch from the pine forests in Tlaxcalan territory.
Tree trunks were slashed, and the pitch that oozed out was collected
in cups. When the oozing stopped, the trees were chopped into logs and
burned in piles over depressions in the earth. Tar collected in the
depressions and was removed after several days.

In Europe, beef tallow would have been mixed with the pine
resins, but in Mexico there were no cattle. This deficiency was made
up by human fat. Because the Spaniards and their allies were con-
stantly skirmishing with the Aztecs, there were plenty of bodies to
supply it. Some Spaniards tried to cover up this grisly story, and those

who reported it were quick to say the heathenish Indians did all the butchering and the Spaniards only supervised the repugnant task. But in an unrelated anecdote, Díaz nonchalantly tells of cutting open a rotund Indian he had killed to get fat to dress wounds, so butchering humans was not foreign to the conquistadors. As usual, we don't know exactly what Cabrillo did during this gory process, but he may have done more than just supervise it.

Once the ships were built, they were disassembled and carried by slaves to a location near Lake Texcoco that was controlled by Texcocan Indians friendly to Cortés. There, the ships were reassembled and the seams painted with Cabrillo's sealer. Although it would have been simpler to reassemble the *bergantines* on the shore of Lake Texcoco where they were to be used, Aztecs patrolled the lake and would have attacked the shipbuilders. Inland they were safer, but to launch the ships, a canal had to be dug connecting the construction site with the lake. This project employed 40,000 Texcocans, working in 8,000-man shifts for seven weeks. The result was a canal approximately 1.5 miles long with a width and average depth of 12 feet.

Exact descriptions of the *bergantines* are missing, but there is enough information available to get a good picture of what they were like. They and the canals were planned together so that the ships would fit in the waterway. C. Henry Gardiner, author of *Naval Power in the Conquest of Mexico*, believes 12 of the ships were 42 feet long while the flagship was 48 feet. The ships were very narrow—between 8 and 9 feet wide—and barely wide enough to accommodate a double row of oarsmen (six on each side) and leave a passage for soldiers. To get through the canal, the ships were designed to be paddled, rather than

The Aztecs left several drawings of the Spanish bergantines. *Above, Cortés and Doña Marina ride in one accompanied by some native allies. On the facing page, a fleet of* bergantines *attacks Tenochtitlán.*

rowed. Instead of using long, sweeping oars, the men used short, stubby paddles and probably stood up while paddling. The ships were also equipped with square sails. Half had two masts, and half had only one. The vessels were entirely decked, with two small platforms, called castles, rising at either end. Castles were designed as shooting platforms, and the forecastle of each *bergantín* held a heavy gun. The ships probably also had reinforced bulkheads for ramming. Since they were much larger than the Aztec canoes, ramming would have been an effective tactic.

Twenty-five men were assigned to each ship, a balanced complement of crossbowmen, arquebusiers, and infantrymen. The paddlers were soldiers too, who could man their arms when they weren't paddling. Cortés put such faith in the impact of his waterborne contingent that he stationed approximately three-quarters of his artillery and two-thirds of his crossbowmen and arquebusiers on the ships.

On April 28, 1521, the *bergantines* were launched, and on May 21, the siege of Tenochtitlán, the final stage in the conquest of the Aztecs, began. According to Díaz, the Spanish army now consisted of 84 horsemen, 650 soldiers, and 194 crossbowmen. According to Cortés, they were accompanied by at least 150,000 Indian allies who were sick of the Aztecs' rule. This massive force surrounded the city and slowly destroyed it.

The first step was to get control of the lake. The *bergantines*

advanced into Lake Texcoco and engaged the huge fleet of Aztec
canoes, while Cortés's land forces, which were broken into several
armies, took up their positions around Tenochtitlán. After the ships
had made a considerable dent in the canoe force, Cortés split up the
bergantines and assigned them to support the various land forces.
Although the shipborne soldiers couldn't help the fighting within the
city itself, they could guard Spanish encampments from canoe attack
and the ships served as temporary bridges in gaps in the causeways.
The *bergantines* were also the right height to allow their soldiers to
attack Aztecs on the causeway.

Despite the advantage the ships gave them, the Spaniards again suffered terrible losses. The Aztecs fought savagely and forced the Spaniards to enter Tenochtitlán each day where the confined spaces made cannons and horses of little use. Using their temples and palaces as forts, the Aztecs vowed to win or die. Most of the conquistadors, including Cabrillo, were wounded. Díaz reports receiving four wounds and nearly being captured. With regret, Cortés decided he had to level Tenochtitlán. Building by beautiful building, the conquistadors and their allies reduced the Aztec capital to rubble. They also blockaded the Aztec food supply, starving the Indians who were already weakened by an outbreak of illness.

Despite repeated entreaties to surrender (even Cortés hated to destroy these proud people), the Aztecs continued to fight from dawn to dusk for nearly 85 days. Finally, when their leader, Cuauhtémoc, Montezuma's nephew, was captured, the siege ended. Cortés allowed the few remaining Aztecs to escape into the countryside, but he kept the royal family prisoners.

The Spaniards celebrated their victory with such licentious debauchery that their priest cautioned them against God's wrath. The next day they held a service to thank God for their victory over such a barbaric nation.

The treasure was disappointing for the soldiers. Although Díaz describes it at one point as 700,000 gold dollars, after the royal fifth and Cortés's share were removed, the average soldier ended up with only about 100 dollars, and most of them quickly gambled that away.

After the excitement of victory wore off, the Spanish soldiers grew restless. Discontentment with Cortés and his empty promises to make them rich began to boil. Ever resourceful, their leader came up with the perfect solution—he sent them off to seek more treasure.

The glyph for Cuauhtémoc, last ruler of the Aztec empire.

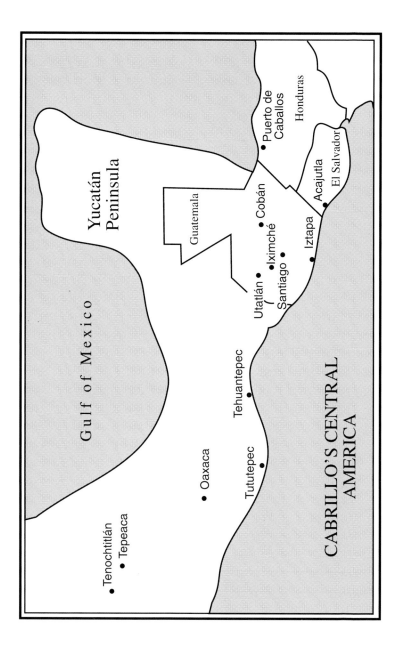

5

On to Central America

Pedro de Alvarado...swept southward
like a whirlwind.
—Hubert Howe Bancroft, historian

During the siege of Mexico, Cortés had learned that the Pacific Ocean was nearby. He and his contemporaries confused the Pacific (or the South Sea as they called it) with the Indian Ocean and believed the lands rimming the Pacific were the Indies, or at least an extension of them. They expected these lands to be teeming with spice and treasure. After Mexico fell, Cortés sent several armies to explore these possibilities, and Juan Rodríguez Cabrillo was assigned to one of them. In October 1521 he joined the army of Francisco de Orozco which had been ordered to explore south of Tepeaca and to subdue the Mixtec Indians of Oaxaca who were causing trouble.

Cabrillo was now a mounted officer in his early 20s, serving, according to records, with "his person, arms, and horse"—the terms used to describe an *hidalgo*. It appears that while many of his compatriots were squandering their money, he had used his wisely. Horses were still rare and expensive in the New World (Columbus had only introduced them to America less than 30 years previously), yet after the Aztec conquest, Cabrillo was able to buy and maintain one. Cabrillo had moved beyond his companions in other ways too. While the majority of the tattered remnants of Narváez's troops had retreated to safety in Cuba after *La Noche Triste*, Cabrillo had returned to Tenochtitlán and fought in the final campaign. By this point in his life, he was a classic conquistador—a courageous and skillful soldier dedicated to seeking adventure.

In Orozco's army, Cabrillo was one of a cocky band of conquistadors made confident by their victory over the Aztecs. Their current target, the Mixtecs, had once been a powerful nation, but by the 16th century their civilization was in decline. After the Spaniards surrounded their capital and blockaded their food supply, the hungry Mixtecs surrendered and became subjects of the Spanish crown. Oaxaca's gold-rich streams and fertile fields appealed to the Spaniards, and several settled on *encomiendas* near the town of Oaxaca. Cabrillo was offered an *encomienda* in this lovely territory, but he refused it. Who knew what lay beyond the next horizon?

War wasn't always necessary to subjugate the natives of Mexico and Central America. The peoples south of the Aztec empire had heard of the powerful Spanish army and knew it was headed in their direction. To avoid being massacred, the poorer and weaker pueblos sent emissaries to Cortés, vowing allegiance to the Spanish king. The stronger and wealthier Indians strengthened their defenses and prepared for war.

Those who promised loyalty to Spain expected the Spaniards to protect them from their neighbors. War and rivalry were so common among the Indians that it wasn't long before Cortés received a call for help from one of his new allies. The ruler of Tehuantepec, on the south coast of Mexico, wanted help fighting his western neighbors, the Tututepecs. In 1522 Pedro de Alvarado was sent to take care of the problem. Cabrillo was in his army.

Alvarado was a handsome man with a deceptively cheerful countenance that hid a violent temperament. The Aztecs called him Tonatiuh, the sun god, for his bright blond hair and dramatic behavior. A man of action and courage, he was an exceptionally capable soldier, whose value in battle kept him from being hanged for his intemperate judgment. As he had proven in the massacre of Aztec nobles that started the Aztec revolt, Alvarado was impulsive, greedy, and chillingly cruel. Prescott says, "He was altogether destitute of...moderation."

With the aid of a large band of Mexican allies, the Spaniards easily overwhelmed the natives of Tututepec. The subdued tribe showered gifts on the conquistadors, including a pair of solid gold stirrups for

*Coat of arms of the
city of Oaxaca.*

Alvarado. Alvarado, however, wasn't satisfied and jailed the chief to collect more gold. Even after the natives had paid a royal ransom, Alvarado let the poor man die in jail, infuriating the natives. Alvarado made more enemies by cheating some of his men out of gold that was rightfully theirs. Then he left Segura, the town he had founded in the Tututepec region, in their hands and returned to Tenochtitlán, accompanied by Cabrillo.

Not surprisingly, Segura disintegrated. Many Spaniards left, and those who stayed were attacked by natives seeking revenge for Alvarado's atrocities. When Alvarado heard of the rebellion, he returned with an army, which included Cabrillo, and quelled the revolt.

While in the land of the Tututepecs, Alvarado heard of tribes with splendid treasures in Guatemala and Honduras. In December, with permission from Cortés, he traveled to Guatemala to conquer the natives. His army consisted of 120 horsemen, 300 foot soldiers, and a large band of Tlaxcalans. Cabrillo was now one of Alvarado's main captains. He would spend the next 12 years serving this mercurial man in the wilds of Guatemala and Honduras.

The geography of Guatemala is marked by high, volcanically active mountains, deep ravines, icy cold streams, thick jungles, and steaming swamps. Lush tropical plants tumble over the landscape, creating a wild beauty that's nearly impassable. The Spaniards' progress through this terrain was arduous. In fact, historian Hubert Howe Bancroft wrote in the late 1800s, "So severe were [the Spaniards'] struggles with nature and Satan, to whom these stubborn soldiers ascribed most ills, that their former troubles seemed to them as pastime now."

As if the landscape wasn't trouble enough, the soldiers also had to fight Indians at every step. The natives of Guatemala were remnants

of the Mayan civilization, a complex society that historians believe at its peak was more advanced than that of the Aztecs or the Incas of Peru. For some reason, around the ninth century B.C., the Mayas migrated north to the Yucatán peninsula where their civilization declined. A few Mayan tribes remained in Central America, and these were the Indians the Spanish encountered. No longer highly civilized, they were fiercely independent and quick to fight to defend their land.

To each of these tribes, Alvarado sent emissaries who, according to Bancroft, told the Mayas "they had come from the emperor of the world, and from his invincible captain, who, though no god, had found his way hither to show them the path to paradise." All they had to do to receive this magnanimous gift was vow allegiance to the Spanish crown. A few years earlier, more tribes might have laughed at this offer, but one-third of the natives of the Guatemala Highlands had been wiped out by smallpox brought by earlier European scouts. Thus weakened, the Cakchiquels, one of the largest Mayan tribes, quickly submitted to Spanish rule in exchange for help fighting their enemies—two other major Mayan groups called the Quichés and the Tzutuhils.

Alvarado took on the Quichés first. The mountainous terrain made fighting extremely difficult because the Spaniards needed flat, open land for their artillery and horses to be effective. However, after a number of savage battles, the Quichés surrendered and invited the Spaniards to a conciliatory feast in Utatlán, their capital. Utatlán rivaled Tenochtitlán for beauty, wealth, and limited accessibility. Surrounded by a ravine, it was accessible only by a drawbridge and a perilous footpath up the vertical face of the ravine. Utatlán was suspiciously quiet and empty of natives when the Spaniards arrived. Sensing a trap, Alvarado ordered his army to retreat. The last horse and rider barely made it across the drawbridge before it became too weak to hold them; the Indians had cut the bridge supports as part of a plan to trap the Spaniards and then burn them in the city. Alvarado's vengeance was swift and terrible. He burned the Quiché king and nobles and then destroyed Utatlán.

In April 1524, Alvarado's army, reinforced by Cakchiquels, set out to subdue the Tzutuhils. In a battle against 16,000 Tzutuhils, Alvarado won another decisive victory.

The triumphant army returned to its home base in Iximché, the Cakchiquel capital, and on July 25, 1524, Alvarado proclaimed the conquest of Guatemala officially complete. He made Iximché the capital, renaming it Ciudad del Señor Santiago. On August 12, Santiago's official citizens signed the city's register. Cabrillo, still known as Juan Rodríguez, was 29th on the list. Santiago remained a rude camp of grass and mud huts for several years.

Many natives despised the Spaniards and resisted their attempts to control them. By 1525, the Cakchiquels had become so disenchanted with their guests that they too attacked the Spanish encampment and forced them to relocate Santiago. In 1527, another battle caused Santiago to be moved again.

For the next several years, Spanish armies marched back and forth across Guatemala, Honduras, and El Salvador, quelling one uprising after another. Because of the tortuous terrain, in some areas clear victories were impossible. The Indians simply melted into the mountains or jungle only to rise again when the Spaniards were gone. Despite this, the army conquered large tracts of land and captured natives to work in the gold fields of Guatemala. Guatemala's streams contained rich gold deposits, and, as in Cuba, many natives died of exposure and starvation mining gold for the Europeans.

Defeated Indian tribes also supplied women to the Spaniards. Most of these liaisons were brief. As Bancroft explains, to the Spaniards gold was to keep, and "women were to use and throw away." But occasionally a relationship lasted. Sometime during the early campaigns in Guatemala, Cabrillo and some of his companions took Indian wives. The name and tribe of Cabrillo's wife aren't known, but over several years she bore him at least three daughters, all of whom would marry conquistadors.

Alvarado in the Guatemala campaign.

In 1526, Alvarado was called to Honduras to help Cortés battle insurgents. Cristóbal de Olid, who had been one of Cortés's trusted captains, was trying to claim Honduras for himself. After Olid was hanged and Honduras resecured, both Cortés and Alvarado were swept into a struggle for control of New Spain, as Mexico was now called.

Enemies of Cortés, who were jealous of his wealth and power (the king had made him governor and captain-general of New Spain), took advantage of his absence in Honduras to usurp his power and discredit him with the king. They said Cortés was planning to take Mexico from Spain and make it his own kingdom. Cortés undoubtedly had enough power and supporters to do just that, but records indicate he remained dutifully loyal to the crown. As a follower of Cortés, Alvarado was also accused of crimes against the crown. Eventually both he and Cortés would journey separately to Spain to defend themselves before the king. Alvarado would not return to Guatemala until 1530.

While he was away, two of his brothers and an official sent by the anti-Cortés group in Mexico served in turn as acting lieutenant governor of Guatemala. Their combined misadministration increased the Indian uprisings and split the Spanish residents into bickering factions. Favoritism shown some of the citizens by the acting officials caused the division.

While Jorge Alvarado was acting lieutenant governor, disagreements arose when he tried to collect back taxes from the citizens of Santiago. Tired of living in a city that was nothing but a crude, mobile camp, they refused to pay until a permanent city was established. Many had been fighting in the New World for more than 10 years and were ready to settle down in the city they had been promised as payment for their service. Jorge agreed to their demands, setting off another dispute—this time over the location of the city.

According to Bancroft, most of the people wanted a site in the Almolonga Valley which had "a cool and healthful climate, a plentiful supply of wood, water, and pasture, and where the slope of the ground would allow the streets to be cleansed by the periodical rains." Others sided with Hernando de Alvarado, another brother of Pedro, who called the Almolonga site "a land of volcanoes and sandstone, where the earth trembles greatly because of the fire belching from the volcanoes." Hernando favored a different location, but he was out-voted.

On November 22, 1527, Santiago was reestablished at the site of an old Indian village in the Valley of Almolonga. The name Juan Rodríguez appears with 20 others on the list of official citizens. These were the only people entitled to own land, and they had earned this privilege through their service in the army.

The volcano Hunaphu towered over Santiago. Cloaked by a thick blanket of palms, pines, and ferns, it suited its Indian name, which means mountain of rich greenery. Over centuries, Hunaphu's crater had become a lake filled with rainwater. It would play an important part in the future of Santiago.

In the fertile valley, the conquistadors laid out Santiago according to Spanish ordinances for New World cities. Around a central plaza they built a church and the governor's palace. Locations were assigned for a hospital, chapel and shrine, a fortress, municipal and civic buildings, and a prison. A district of fine homes for the wealthier citizens was constructed, and the Mexican Indian allies who continued to serve the Spaniards built their own settlement outside the city. Public buildings were constructed of stone, while most homes were adobe or mud and cane. Roofs were thatched.

Depending on rank and distinction of service, soldiers received different sized *solares*, or house lots. As a horseman, Cabrillo received a 600x300-foot *solare*, while that of a foot soldier was 300x150 feet. Horsemen also received a lot 600x1,400 paces for farming and grazing. So prosperous was Santiago, that within six months, 150 names were added to the community list. And within a year, Bancroft writes, "the town was surrounded with cornfields and orchards, and the valley of Almolonga soon became one of the most flourishing colonies throughout the breadth of Central America."

Cabrillo settled in Santiago and became one of its richest citizens. Along with the land he was entitled to as a soldier, he received several *encomiendas* for his service to the crown. In 1529, he and two friends—Diego Sánchez de Ortega and Sancho de Barahona—received permission to look for gold while the other soldiers were restricted to Santiago and military duty. This special treatment may have been the result of the favoritism practiced by one of the interim lieutenant governors. Whatever its source, Cabrillo was clearly a privileged citizen of Guatemala.

The trio's gold hunting paid off royally with the discovery of Cobán, a gold-rich pueblo north of Santiago. Cobán's gold was located along streams in gravel deposits called placers. It was mined for the Spaniards by natives who panned for it using wooden bowls called *bateas*. Supporting the mining process exacted a heavy toll on the natives of Cobán, who not only had to supply the panners, but also those who dug gravel, carried supplies, and performed domestic chores. In addition, they had to produce the chicken, corn, chiles, honey, and beans all these people ate, and raise money crops, like cacao, which the *encomenderos*, or land owners, sold. Indian managers—usually Mexican natives who looked down on the Guatemalans and treated them accordingly—supervised the *encomiendas*. Cabrillo spent part of each year living on his various properties.

About the time the three gold hunters found Cobán, Pedro de Alvarado returned triumphantly to Guatemala after charming the king of Spain into making him *adelantado*, or governor, of Guatemala. Bancroft reports a rumor that the king, while in his royal gardens, happened to see Alvarado walking by. Struck by the stranger's handsome appearance, the king asked who this man was. When he learned it was Alvarado, he ordered the charges against him dropped. For years Alvarado had begged Cortés to ask the king to reward his service to the crown, but Cortés had dragged his feet, not wishing to share the limelight. Now Alvarado had won his own royal recognition and was finally independent of Cortés.

Cortés had also been vindicated of the charge of disloyalty, and as reward for his phenomenal service to Spain, the king had elevated him to the royal rank of marquess and had granted him a vast tract of land in the valley of Oaxaca, and large estates in and near Mexico City (the fine Spanish capital Cortés was building on the ruins of Tenochtitlán). From now on, he would be known as the Marquess of the Valley. These grants made him by far the wealthiest resident of the New World. The king held back one reward, however. He didn't rename Cortés governor of New Spain. Although Cortés had served admirably in that capacity, establishing remarkably wise policies for the huge new colony, in 1529 the king only reinstated Cortés's military title, Captain-General of New Spain and the coasts of the South Sea. This gave him the right to continue exploring new territory, but civil leadership was passed to others.

Cortés was not happy about losing control of Mexico, but as Prescott explains, Spain traditionally employed "one class of its subjects to effect conquests, and another class to rule over them. For the latter it selected men in whom the fire of ambition was tempered by a cooler judgment....Even Columbus...had not been permitted to preside over the colonies; and still less likely would it be to concede this power to one possessed of the aspiring temper of Cortés." Cortés's star had reached its zenith, but others were rising.

In the early 1530s, news began arriving of another fabulously wealthy civilization, the Incas of Peru. Not one to be left out of plunder, Alvarado, in 1532, assembled a fleet to sail to Peru. Cabrillo, despite his knowledge of shipbuilding, was not involved in this project. He was busy with plans of his own. In 1532, he sailed to Spain to be married.

6

A Man of Means

Juan Rodríguez Cabrillo supported his house, wife, and family, and in the Conquest he served His Majesty with his person, his weapons, his horse, and his retainers, and this was the way he was esteemed in these parts.
—testimony given by Cabrillo's son

Although native wives were fairly common in the early days of Spain's New World colonies, "official" wives were rare. Few single European women lived in the Americas, and most cavaliers were too poor to travel to Mexico, much less Europe, to find a wife.

Cortés was a legendary womanizer whose "activities" made him miss his first sailing date for America while he recovered from injuries inflicted by a lady friend's irate husband. He unwittingly met his first wife, Catalina Xuarez, in Cuba. Her brother-in-law, Cuban governor Velázquez, was so enraged when he learned that Cortés had taken liberties with Catalina and then jilted her, that he jailed Cortés and forced him to marry her.

After the nuptials, Cortés sailed off to Mexico and didn't see his wife again until well after the defeat of the Aztecs. Catalina died soon after their reunion, starting a flurry of rumors that Cortés had poisoned her. Cortés didn't lose himself in grief. In 1529, when he returned in triumph to Spain, he won the hand of Juana de Zuñiga, the niece of the powerful Duke of Bejar. This match lasted. Juana bore him three daughters and a son and managed his household in Mexico.

Pedro de Alvarado also married aristocratic women. After gaining the king's favor in Spain in 1527, he jilted the cousin of Cortés to whom he was betrothed, and wooed and married Francisca de la Cueva, the niece of the Duke of Albuquerque. Francisca died of fever enroute to her new home, but Alvarado later married her sister Beatriz. This union required a special dispensation from the pope—a rare intervention that indicates how popular and powerful Alvarado was. Beatriz was sturdier than her sister and survived the trip to Guatemala, where she became comfortably ensconced in the governor's mansion and eventually succeeded her husband to the governorship.

For those conquistadors who couldn't afford to travel to find a wife, there were native women. But many cavaliers were too proud to legally marry anyone they considered their inferior. These men were in trouble in 1538 when the king ordered all *encomenderos* to marry or lose their property. Alvarado brought 20 single women from Spain to help remedy the situation, but, although all had planned to marry conquistadors, some changed their minds after seeing their battered and aging suitors.

"One would think by the way they are cut up that they just escaped from [hell];" reported one young lady, "for some are lame, some with but one hand, others without ears, others with only one eye, others with half their face gone, and the best of them have one or two cuts across the forehead....Let those wed them who choose, I will not...!"

Other women were more practical. "We are not to marry them for their good looks," said a pragmatic *señorita*, "but for the purpose of inheriting their Indians; for they are so old and worn out that they will soon die, and then we can choose in place of these old men young fellows to our tastes, in the same manner that an old kettle is exchanged for one that is new and sound."

One "old kettle" reportedly overheard this conversation and lost his concern about marrying an inferior. He quickly married a chief's daughter he'd been eyeing.

Cabrillo, however, was neither noticeably disfigured nor poor. In 1532, when he went to Spain to marry, he was in his early thirties and a man of means in Guatemala. Indian uprisings still called him away from Santiago, but for the first time in his adult life he could devote much of his time to his considerable personal business and domestic affairs. Not only was he an *encomendero* of Cobán, but also the owner of a growing number of other *encomiendas*.

The woman he chose to marry was Beatriz Sánchez de Ortega, the sister of Diego Sánchez de Ortega, one of Cabrillo's Cobán partners. Ortega was also the Seville merchant's son whom historian Kelsey speculates may have accompanied Cabrillo to the New World. If Kelsey is correct, Cabrillo may have met Beatriz in Spain before he sailed to Cuba, but it's more likely that Beatriz was the unknown but suitable sister of a friend.

Kelsey suggests that Cabrillo stayed in Europe for as long as a year, wooing Beatriz, visiting family and friends, and buying supplies to take back to Guatemala. Since a great deal of money could be made selling European products in the New World, he probably bought not only what he could use, but also goods he could sell.

Beatriz and Cabrillo were married in Spain in either late 1532 or early 1533 and were back in Santiago by the summer of 1533. The details of their journey aren't known, but even in the best of circumstances travel from Spain to Guatemala was long and arduous. Besides the interminable sea voyage, they endured the perilous trip through the mountains and steamy jungles of Mexico and Guatemala. They probably rode horseback on the open trails and the backs of Indians through the more treacherous passages.

One wonders what Beatriz thought of this journey and of her new home and husband. Although Cabrillo was a wealthy resident and undoubtedly had a fine house, Santiago was still only a small outpost in the wilds of Central America—a far cry from the cosmopolitan city of Seville where Beatriz had grown up.

Cabrillo's home was probably a two-story adobe house with all the rooms opening onto a central courtyard. No matter how large it was, it was undoubtedly crowded. The honor of being a monied *hidalgo* required Cabrillo, and others like him, to house, feed, and protect an assorted group of less-fortunates, called a *casa poblada* or *mucha familia*. Historian Harry Kelsey describes this group as "natural children borne by Indian wives before the arrival of the wife from Spain, poor relatives, impoverished gentlemen, military aides, dependent maiden ladies (either orphans or children of other conquistadors), proteges, friends, Indian servants, and slaves."

The responsibility of caring for all these people was enforceable by law and could weigh heavily on the *hidalgos*. They, in turn, passed the burden along to the natives of their *encomiendas* who had to provide the household servants, food, and housewares needed by their landlord's *casa poblada*. Cobán furnished chickens, maize, chiles, honey, beans, salt, clay pots and griddles for Cabrillo's house. His *encomienda* at Xicalapa contributed fresh fish several times a week, and those at Comitlán and Xocotenango produced chickens, clay pots, and blankets. Some of the management of this complex household would fall upon Beatriz.

None of Cabrillo's contemporaries left written descriptions of his appearance or personality. Cabrillo's own writing is plain and direct and deals with the practical matters of his life, just as those contemporaries who mention him tell only of his skills as a soldier, the head of a *mucha familia*, or as a "man of the sea."

We can guess from these clues that Cabrillo was foremost a practical man who tackled the challenges of life in a businesslike manner. He was literate, but didn't have the fine, flowery literary style of a man with an advanced education. He had the respect of others, for in records, Beatriz and many of his companions refer to the responsible way he fulfilled his duty to family and country. His participation in the brutal treatment of natives doesn't mean he was a particularly cruel or unfeeling individual. Those, like Alvarado, who went out of

Pedro de Alvarado.

their way to be mean are described as such by their peers.   Cabrillo, however, appears to have been a man of his time—believing without question in the superiority of Christians and white men over American natives, and in the white man's manifest destiny to rule over people of color in whatever manner was expedient.

Cabrillo probably had an unremarkable appearance, or the observers of the day would have commented on it. His years of soldiering undoubtedly left him scarred—even the handsome Alvarado had one leg shorter than the other as the result of an Indian's arrow—but his scars weren't disfiguring enough to merit comment.

Not much is known about Beatriz. We do know she couldn't read or write. She and Cabrillo had at least two sons. The first was born in early 1536 and was baptized with his father's name in Santiago's church. The birthdate of the second son, Diego Sánchez de Ortega, is unknown. However, in 1543, a notary in Guatemala recorded that the two boys appeared to be about the same age.

After Cabrillo and Beatriz returned from Spain, Cabrillo began arranging a trading voyage to Peru. Francisco Pizarro, the leader of the Spanish forces trying to conquer the wealthy Incas in Peru, needed supplies to carry on the campaign, and he was willing to pay highly inflated prices. In the port of Acajutla, El Salvador, Cabrillo built a large sailing ship called the *Santiago*. Acajutla was a poor port, open to weather and with a treacherous reef across its mouth, but the other seaport in the area, Iztapa, located about 40 miles south of Santiago, wasn't much better, and it was already occupied with workmen building a fleet for Alvarado.

When the king made Alvarado governor of Guatemala, part of

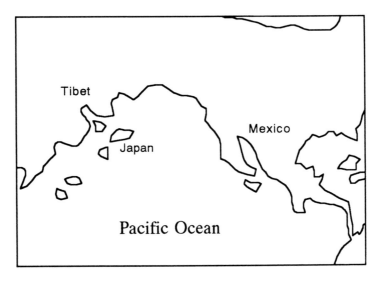

Although Italian cartographer Paulo de Furlani didn't make this map until 1560, it shows the belief also common in the early 1500s that Asia was close to New Spain.

their agreement was that Alvarado would lead voyages of exploration for the crown into the Pacific. By this time, Portugal had become firmly established in India and the Spice Islands (Moluccas), and Spain had given up any claims she had to the Moluccas to save the expense of sending expeditions there (the royal coffers were being drained by war in Europe). However, the Philippines, all the unknown islands of the Pacific, and Asia, which the Spaniards believed were right around the corner from the New World, were still available, and trade routes to these places were sought. The ships Alvarado was building in Iztapa were for this purpose. Cortés and several others received similar royal commissions, heightening the rivalry that already existed among these men.

Whether the king was supposed to reimburse Alvarado for his expenses is unclear. The *adelantado*, or governor, as Alvarado was now known, wrote Charles, saying the cost of building the ships and procuring an army was bankrupting him. When his ships were finished, despite his royal commission, Alvarado couldn't resist the urge to go to Peru and share in the astounding wealth being found there. The treasure of the Incas was even more extensive than that of the Aztecs. Although he'd been warned to stay away from the claims of other Spaniards, Alvarado wrote the king asking for permission to "help" Pizarro conquer the Incas. Months passed before a reply was received. Meanwhile, Alvarado spent vast sums of money maintaining his ships and feeding his army.

Early in 1534, Cabrillo sailed his ship, the *Santiago*, to the Bay of Fonseca in Honduras, where Alvarado had moved his fleet. After delivering some messages, he left quickly. Cabrillo was becoming wary of his commander, who was not to be trusted around property as attractive as the *Santiago*.

Alvarado finally received permission to sail but was told explicitly to travel well south of Pizarro's claim before landing. Not surprisingly, Alvarado didn't do this. Saying the wind forced him ashore, he landed in Ecuador and marched his troops across treacherous, snow-covered mountains to meet with a group from Pizarro's forces. According to Bancroft, this passage was so treacherous that Alvarado left the "entire way strewn with dead." One hundred of his soldiers and 2,000 of his Indian allies died along the way.

Enough of his army remained, however, to sell. The conquistadors of Peru paid 100,000 *castellanos* for Alvarado's remaining men and part of his fleet. Although it's hard to value this amount in today's currency, it was an enormous sum then (the Spanish government in Cabrillo's era figured it cost less than one *castellano* to feed ten sailors for a year), but it barely covered Alvarado's expenses, and when he returned to Guatemala, he discovered that the silver bars he'd been paid with were half copper.

While Alvarado was away, Cabrillo had loaded the *Santiago* with trade goods that he intended to sell in Peru. Altogether, he expected to make 5,000 *castellanos* for this voyage. When Alvarado returned from Peru, he saw the loaded *Santiago*. Whether motivated by his normal greed or disappointment over his Peruvian venture, Alvarado seized Cabrillo's ship and sent it out to explore the South Sea. The *Santiago* was gone for two years. When it returned, its valuable cargo was gone, and it was so "decrepit, old, and broken," according to Cabrillo, that it was worth only 200 *pesos*. Alvarado paid him 150.

Cabrillo tried to collect damages for his lost ship and trade profits, but Alvarado never settled. Instead, he tried to distract Cabrillo by interesting him in plans for a grand new sea adventure he guaranteed would make them both rich. In 1536, however, all plans had to be set aside when a crisis arose in Honduras. The colonists of that colony were a quarreling, greedy, and ineffectual lot who had fractured into tiny settlements too small to support or protect themselves. About to lose Honduras back to the natives, they called on Alvarado to come help them.

In 1536, Alvarado and Cabrillo arrived with an army. The governor of Honduras resigned and gave the burden of the colony's leadership to Alvarado. In situations like this, he was extremely effective. Alvarado reorganized the colonists and quickly put down the rebelling natives.

For his part in the Honduras campaign, Alvarado rewarded "Juan Rodríguez Cabrillo" with "the pueblos Teota and Cotela, with all its señores, Indians, barrios, and fields." The document bearing this proclamation (dated July 20, 1536) was the first in which the name *Cabrillo* appeared linked with *Juan Rodríguez*. Could the recent birth of Cabrillo's heir and namesake have prompted it? In those days, people of means were more likely to have a surname than those of humble origins. Perhaps Cabrillo wanted to give his new family the respectability of a surname. Whatever the reason for the addition, Juan Rodríguez continued to use it during the rest of his life.

After Honduras was secured, Alvarado returned to Spain. Once again he had been accused of mismanaging royal funds and needed to defend himself before the Spanish king. He also sought permission for a new expedition. Before he left for Europe, he appointed Cabrillo *justicia mayor* (chief magistrate) of the seaport Iztapa and ordered him to build a fleet for exploration.

According to Kelsey, "Iztapa was a miserable town." Approximately 40 miles south of Santiago on the Pacific coast, it was a humid place made squalid by the makeshift camps of the thousands of Spaniards and Indians employed in shipbuilding. As a port, it left a great deal to be desired, too. Its shoreline was steep, the tides fast, and the Michatoya River, which entered the sea there, altered the channel with each flood. Timber for shipbuilding, however, was plentiful, and it was the only port in Guatemala.

Cabrillo and his family would live there off and on for the next four years while the fleet was being built. Besides being Iztapa's magistrate, Cabrillo would oversee the entire shipbuilding project—a major undertaking. Whatever was necessary to get the job done, he had the power and ingenuity to make happen.

The ships most commonly used on expeditions during the Age of Exploration were the caravel, top; the carrack, center; and the galleon, bottom.

7

Builder of Ships

The Señor Adelantado...ordered that I should build him an armada while he was in Spain, and so I built it.
—Juan Rodríguez Cabrillo

Shipbuilding in the 16th century was an unpredictable process. The sciences of marine architecture and engineering that would systemize and standardize ship design and construction wouldn't be developed for many decades. The first comprehensive books on these topics wouldn't appear until the end of the next century. As one 16th-century captain put it, "some ships start in the yards as small ones and end as large ones, while others start as large ships and end as small ones." No two were ever the same.

The shipwright's trade was a secretive business with methods and designs jealously guarded and passed from father to son. Construction was usually guided by a master builder, who stuck to a few tried-and-true designs. The quality of his end product depended on his skill, the quality of available materials, and the experience of his workers.

Records of the construction of Alvarado's fleet and shipbuilding in general in early New World colonies are scarce, but it is possible to get an idea of what the process was like. It began with the selection of a slip, or construction site, which ideally was near a good wood supply, far from the gales of the open sea, but near enough to a body of water for easy launching. Cabrillo's slips were at Girabaltique, just up the Michatoya River from Iztapa.

There, skilled workmen set up shops and practiced their various trades. Blacksmiths forged nails, spikes, chains, and bolts from iron imported from Europe. Carpenters, shipwrights, and sawyers worked with wood. Some guided its selection and cutting in the nearby forests where Indians provided the labor. Back at the slip, the keel or backbone of each ship was carefully hewed, and the stern post, stem post, and ribs attached to it. Crossbeams and wooden "knees" held the skeleton together, while the ships were kept upright by blocks and shoring. Scaffolding around each hull provided working platforms for the shipwrights.

Planks for the deck and hull were screwed or nailed edge to edge along the frame in a manner of construction called carvel. Fastenings were made of iron or wood. Wooden pegs were favored in areas below water where they would swell and hold tightly. Workers drove a caulking mixture of hemp fibers and pitch into the gaps between the boards, and they painted the infamous tallow and pitch mixture onto the outside of the hull to keep sea worms at bay. When the hull was complete, the ship was launched at high tide. In some cases, the hull rested on wooden ways leading to the river. When it was time to launch, the ways were greased, shoring removed, and the ship slid into the river. Ballasting, masting, and rigging remained to be done.

Ballast, in the form of sand and rocks, was loaded into unused portions of the hold to stabilize the buoyant hull. It would be adjusted later for each voyage, depending on the cargo. While the masts were being shaped, their bottom, or heel, was squared off to fit into a square frame in the hull called a step. The step kept the mast from rotating. Erecting the mast was called stepping it. In Cabrillo's time, rigging was made of hemp, and sails were either woven linen or canvas. Both were expensive. Each ship was also fitted out with innumerable pieces of equipment, ranging from anchors to hourglasses, cooking pots, and casks. Alvarado's fleet also carried impressive armories of weapons.

Although the shipbuilding techniques of Cabrillo's day were relatively simple, the construction of these seven or eight ships (the exact number is unclear) was a phenomenal task. Some say it cost as much money as 80 ships would have in Spain, and we know it took a huge toll in human suffering. The natives of Central America and blacks imported from Africa bore the brunt of the work.

The most devastating task was the transportation of supplies. In

1539, when Alvarado returned from Spain, he brought three ships full of marine equipment, weapons, and supplies. Whole regions of Guatemala and Honduras were stripped of their natives to transport this cargo the approximately 325 miles from Puerto de Caballos on the Atlantic coast of Honduras to Iztapa and Acajutla (where the final fitting out was done) on the Pacific. Roped together like oxen, thousands of natives carried or dragged their heavy burdens through jungles and across mountains. Father Bartolomé de las Casas, frustrated protector of New World natives, painted a graphic picture of Alvarado's convoy in a report to the king, "Anchors cut furrows into the shoulders and loins of some of...the sad, naked people," he wrote, and many died from exhaustion along the way. Altogether, he said, Alvarado "killed an infinite number of people building the ships."

Indians also supplied and prepared the large quantities of food consumed by the work crews, and even the Tlaxcalan warriors, who ordinarily only oversaw the Guatemalan Indians, were forced to perform heavy manual labor.

The work was hard, and the hot, humid conditions oppressive. Primitive Iztapa offered no entertainment, and the white workers grew rebellious. (The natives and blacks were probably too exhausted and well-guarded to rebel.) To pacify the Europeans, *Justicia Mayor* Cabrillo imported Indian women to warm their beds and work as household servants. The new bishop of Santiago, Francisco Marroquín, was scandalized by this "abominable affair," and wrote King Charles to stop it. However, before the king could respond, the fleet was done.

Wherever and however Cabrillo learned about shipbuilding, he had become a master of his profession. Observers of the day wrote that this was the best fleet on the Pacific. Even Bishop Marroquín recalled

*Two 15th-century shipbuilders shape a timber in this drawing
adapted from the Nuremberg Chronicles.*

later that it was "the largest and best to sail the Mar del Sur [Pacific]
up to that time and for many years thereafter."

The fleet contained the ships built at Iztapa and several others
purchased by Alvarado. One was the *Santiago*, Cabrillo's first vessel,
which Alvarado had commandeered and ruined. At Alvarado's request, Cabrillo replanked and refitted it, making it once again a fine
ship. Cabrillo also built a new sailing vessel for himself. Officially
called the *San Salvador*, it was commonly known as the *Juan Rodríguez*
for its owner, as was the custom in those days. Several other citizens
added private vessels to the fleet, hoping to get rich selling trade goods
along the way. Altogether, there were 13 ships. Most were either built
or fitted out by Cabrillo.

Historians and sailing-ship buffs have argued for decades over the
exact description of this fleet. What types of ships did it include, and
how big were they? What was their sail configuration, and how many
had oars? Heated debate continues, and many questions remain
unanswered. Alvarado commissioned a painting of the fleet, but it as
well as an official written description have been lost. Existing references come from eyewitness accounts, but they conflict and are
confusing.

One problem comes from their language. Words used to describe
ships differed from one century to another and from one country to
another. In the time of Charles V, a frigate was a small vessel with only
a partial deck, but 300 years later, a frigate was a major ship of up to
2,000 tons. Historians through the centuries didn't keep the various
meanings straight, and experts today still disagree on the terms. What

one person calls a *nao*, another calls a carrack. What somebody else identifies as a galleon, others call a caravel. Also, it's probable that due to the idiosyncracies of shipbuilding in the 16th century, ships, including Alvarado's, were not pure examples of any formal ship type. So it's impossible to arrive at a description of Alvarado's fleet that everyone agrees with. However, between the eyewitness accounts and what is known about ships of that era, it's possible to get an idea of what the vessels were like.

Experts generally agree that of the 13 ships in Alvarado's fleet, three were large, seven were medium sized, and three were small. Some historians call the three large ships caravels; others call them galleons. Oviedo, the official historian of the Indies at that time, wrote that the three were 200 *toneladas* each in size. (The *tonelada*—also called a tun or ton—was a measurement used to indicate a ship's carrying capacity below deck. Based on the size of a wine tun, a large cask used to transport wine, it was very roughly 40 cubic feet.) Other sources indicate each of the largest ships had at least two decks, which some people interpret to mean that they had fore- and sterncastles. (These structures were originally temporary platforms built at the front and back of ships for soldiers to shoot from. Over time they became permanent, reaching great heights and extending to form full and partial decks.) Cabrillo's ships, the *Santiago* and *San Salvador,* were two of the three large ships of the fleet, and Kelsey speculates the *Diosdado*, a private merchant vessel, was the third. He also estimates they were approximately 100 feet long and 25 feet wide. Melbourne Smith, a current world-renowned ship reconstructionist, believes the *San Salvador* was a galleon.

The following definitions come from *The Oxford Companion to Ships & the Sea*, edited by Peter Kemp, Oxford University Press, 1976. Caravels were the premiere ships of discovery during the early days of the Age of Exploration. Developed by the Portuguese, the caravel had a shallow draft and was relatively small (not longer than 100 feet and usually between 75 and 80 feet), which made it perfect for exploring coastal waters. It was also easy to handle and required only a small crew. But what made the Portuguese boast that the caravel was "a ship for coming home," was its ability to carry both square and triangular (or lateen) sails. This innovation allowed crews to take advantage of the strengths both types of sails offered.

When the wind blows from behind a ship, square sails allow the ship to go faster than triangular sails. But when the wind comes from the direction the crew wants to go, triangular sails allow the vessel to sail more closely into the wind. All sailing ships have to tack, or sail a zig-zag course into the wind, but triangular sails allow ships to sail within approximately 55° of the wind, while square rigs can only approach 67°. Before this development, explorers were prevented by their ships from exploring areas of the world with predominantly unfavorable winds. An example is the west coast of Africa. Until the advent of the caravel, European explorers were hesitant to investigate that coast, because, although it was possible to sail down it, returning north against that coast's fierce north winds was nearly impossible. (Cabrillo would face the same situation along the west coast of North America.) Galleons, which were developed after the caravel, could sail even more efficiently against the wind. Slightly larger and more streamlined than the caravel, they also had more enclosed deck space, and could carry more cargo.

Kelsey believes the seven medium-sized ships in Cabrillo's fleet were between 100 and 150 *toneladas*, which concurs with Oviedo's report that they were 100 *toneladas* or more, and Kelsey calls them uncastled carracks. Alvarado called them *naos gruesas*, or big-bellied ships. Traditionally the carrack (also known as a *nao, nef*, or fully-rigged ship) is thought to have been larger than the caravel or galleon and equipped with tall fore- and sterncastles, which doesn't match Kelsey's description. However, carracks did have a larger carrying capacity than caravels or galleons, which agrees with Alvarado's description that the seven ships were big bellied. Carracks historically were used as much for trade as discovery. Similar to caravels in other ways, they were longer and wider and had more sails to propel their bulk. The carracks in Cabrillo's fleet were the *San Jorge, San Antonio, San Francisco, San Juan de Letrán, Figueroa, Anton Hernández,* and *Alvar Núñez*.

Of the three remaining vessels in the fleet, one was a galley—an oared ship common in the Mediterranean. Alvarado's galley was called the *San Cristóbal*, and Oviedo described it as "very beautiful." The next was the *San Martin*—a *galeota*, or small galley—propelled by a sail and 20 pairs of oars. The final member of Alvarado's fleet was the *San Miguel*, a *bergantín* with 13 pairs of oars and a sail. Used as service vessels, these small boats carried crew members back and forth from ship to shore and towed the big ships in and out of port.

All the ships were square-rigged and may have used lateen sails on their mizzenmasts. Of the 13, Cabrillo is known to have built the *Santiago*, *San Salvador*, and six or seven others.

When the fleet neared completion, Alvarado moved it to Acajutla, El Salvador, for final fitting out. The *San Salvador* was done early, allowing Cabrillo time to make a lucrative trading voyage to Peru before the rest of the fleet was finished. But by late summer 1540, they were all assembled and ready to sail. Alvarado initially had planned to explore the islands between New Spain and China, but while he was in Spain during the previous year, rumors of a new treasure in the New World reached the Spanish court, and his commission was altered to allow him to look for it. This time the treasure was believed to be in the great "Northern Mystery"—the vast and mostly unexplored tract of America north of the Spanish colonies. Therefore, when Alvarado's ships were done, he sailed north from Acajutla harbor to explore the Pacific coast.

Surprisingly, Cabrillo had not planned personally to go along. But as he explained in a legal document, Alvarado "kept after me often begging me that I should come with him in my ship as *almirante* [second in command] of the armada." So, at the last minute, he changed his mind and agreed to join the expedition as captain of the *San Salvador* and *almirante* of the fleet. This was the beginning of the enterprise that led to Cabrillo's own voyage of discovery.

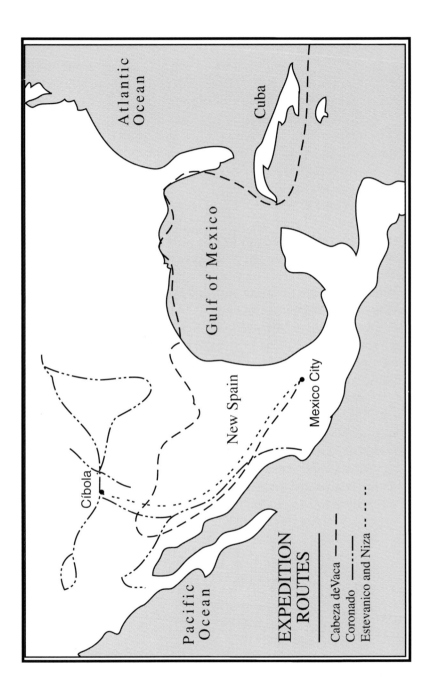

EXPEDITION
ROUTES

Cabeza deVaca — — —
Coronado ——————
Estevanico and Niza ·· — ··

Atlantic
Ocean

Cuba

Gulf of Mexico

New Spain

Mexico City

Cibola

Pacific
Ocean

8

Legends and Myths

Know that on the right hand of the Indies there is an island called California, very close to the side of the Terrestrial Paradise....

—from *The Exploits of Esplandian*, an
early 16th-century romance novel

Cabrillo may have been reluctant to join the expedition, but his hesitancy was undoubtedly not caused by doubt over the existence of more wealthy native civilizations. Tenochtitlán and the Inca empire had proven such places existed, and the legends and romance novels that encouraged Europeans to seek wondrous lands in the first place implied more would be found. New World adventurers would energetically chase rumors of riches until the mid-1540s before it would become clear no more were to be found.

The rumor that excited New World colonists in the late 1530s came from members of an expedition begun by Cortés's old nemesis, Pánfilo de Narváez. Cortés had left the old bungler minus an eye and imprisoned in Mexico in 1520. After three years, Narváez was released and returned to Spain. There he managed to convince the king to name him governor of Florida, which at that time extended from the Florida peninsula west to present-day Texas. Ponce de Leon had discovered Florida in 1513 while searching for the Fountain of Youth, but few Europeans had visited the area since then.

With a force of roughly 600 men and 42 horses, Narváez landed on the west coast of Florida in 1528. Among other things, he was seeking a land of treasure he'd heard of called Appalachee. Narváez commanded his ships to explore the coast while he and his army traveled inland. Against the advice of his officers, he failed to arrange a rendezvous with his ships. After a few equally unwise decisions, he and his men were near starvation and dwindling rapidly in number. The piteously poor natives of Florida were no help, and Narváez's ships had sailed to Cuba after failing to find their commander.

Out of desperation, Narváez and his men killed and ate their horses and made canoes from the skins. They hoped to reach New Spain by sailing along the coast of the Gulf of Mexico. Many men, including Narváez, died during the journey, and the remainder were washed up by a storm on present-day Galveston Island. A bitterly cold winter killed all but six of the tattered survivors, and those wretched fellows were enslaved by Indians. Soon only four remained.

For several years, the four labored under miserable conditions until Alvar Núñez Cabeza de Vaca, the sole surviving officer, gained recognition as a medicine man by healing some of his captors. As a result, he was given relative freedom, and together with the other survivors, he escaped and journeyed on foot across Texas and northern Mexico. In 1536, eight years after landing in Florida, they wandered into the Spanish town of Culiácan in northwest Mexico.

There, and in Mexico City, Cabeza de Vaca told of their phenomenal odyssey. Although he was honest about the hardships they endured and the poverty of the Indians they met, when he mentioned hearing his captors tell of fantastically wealthy cities to the north, he ignited gold fever among the Spaniards. Rumors spread like wildfire. People said Cabeza de Vaca had seen houses filled with gold and knew where to find the golden Seven Cities of Cíbola made famous in a Spanish legend.

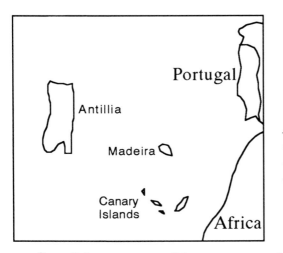

The mythical island of Antillia appears alongside real landmarks in this simplified version of a 1424 chart.

One of the most powerful men to respond to Cabeza de Vaca's story was the first viceroy of New Spain, Antonio de Mendoza. Mendoza was a man "in whom the fire of ambition was tempered by a cooler judgment." King Charles had chosen him to govern New Spain after passing over Cortés. A wise and capable leader, Mendoza did much to help the colony, but he was not above lining his pockets when the opportunity arose.

After listening to Cabeza de Vaca, Mendoza organized a land expedition led by Fray Marcos de Niza and guided by Estevanico, a black slave who had survived the Narváez expedition and who had been Cabeza de Vaca's personal servant (Cabeza de Vaca sold him to Mendoza). Their job was to find the Seven Cities, pacify the natives, and pave the way for a colony.

The legend of the Seven Cities of Cíbola had its roots in the Moors' eighth-century invasion of Iberia. At that time seven Portuguese bishops were believed to have set sail for the mysterious island of Antillia where they intended to establish a colony to preserve Christianity. Down through the centuries, various sightings of the island or its inhabitants were recorded, making the legend more and more believable. Columbus's notebooks indicate he believed in it, and he named the islands he first encountered in the New World the Greater Antilles. Toscanelli, a famous cosmographer of Columbus's era, wrote unequivocally, "From the island Antillia, which you call the Isle

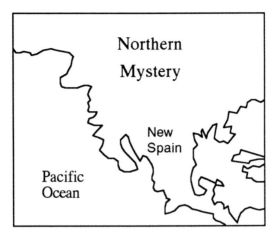

of Seven Cities...to the most noble island of Cipango [Japan] is fifty degrees of longitude." And even Portuguese King João II, grandnephew of Henry the Navigator, sent explorers to find "a large island, islands, or mainland, beyond our shores, presumed to be the island of the Seven Cities."

Each time the cities were reported to have been seen, the riches attributed to them grew. In 1447, the crew of a caravel told of landing on an uncharted island with seven Portuguese-speaking communities and sand streaked with gold. In time, the cities' buildings and streets were said to be gilded. As the Atlantic became more known and Antillia wasn't found, the location of the cities moved westward. In the 16th century, even men as well-educated and sophisticated as Mendoza were ready to believe the cities might exist in the Northern Mystery— the areas of North America as yet unexplored by Europeans.

The expedition Mendoza sent to find the cities was troubled from its start. Making up for his years in captivity, Estevanico had become eccentric and demanding, adorning himself with plumes and tur- quoises and collecting a retinue of Indian servants. Some carried him on a litter, while others bore the special green crockery he used and from which no one else was allowed to eat. Two greyhounds completed his entourage.

The austere and slow-moving Fray Marcos was no match for the flamboyant slave, and the two soon parted company. But before he left, Estevanico agreed to send back wooden crosses of various sizes to indicate what he'd found. A cross the size of a hand would mean a noteworthy discovery. One twice that size would mean a special finding like a large city. Within four days, one of Estevanico's servants returned, bearing a cross the size of a man. He said Estevanico had found "Cíbola," the first of the Seven Cities. Excited by the news, Fray Marcos hurried ahead only to learn Estevanico was dead. The "Cíbolans" had killed him after not taking kindly to his demands for their food and women.

Details of the story grow sketchy here. Fray Marcos returned to Mexico City and told Mendoza he had seen a city that was bigger than Tenochtitlán and that had many-storied buildings with walls made of gold. Historians speculate he actually saw Hawikuh, a Zuñi pueblo in New Mexico. Not wishing to meet Estevanico's fate, Fray Marcos undoubtedly kept his distance from the pueblo, but to a friar with a good imagination, it may well have looked bigger than the Aztec capital, and washed with sunlight, the walls may well have looked like gold.

Fray Marcos's report heightened the colonists' zeal to find the Seven Cities, and it intensified the rivalry among New Spain's chief explorers—Alvarado, Cortés, and Mendoza—to find them. In 1540, on the strength of Marcos's account, Mendoza sent Francisco Vásquez de Coronado with 2,000 men to visit Cíbola. When Coronado reached the pueblo, he would have wrung Fray Marcos's neck if the good friar had been present. Cíbola was small, rundown, and very poor. Despite this evidence, Coronado had a hard time giving up his belief in the Seven Cities. He would spend the next two years exploring from the Colorado River to Kansas, checking out any rumors of gold he heard until he finally realized his search was fruitless.

Cortés had begun exploring the Pacific coast north of New Spain well before the rumors of the Seven Cities had begun. Drawing on his success at building ships for the conquest of Tenochtitlán, he had built several ships for exploration on the west coast of New Spain before Alvarado had started his ship construction enterprises. Looking for a route to the Orient, Cortés had sent several expeditions between 1532 and 1536 to explore the then-untraversed Gulf of California. One landed near the southern tip of Baja, or Lower California, and claimed it for Spain, thinking it was one of the islands close to the Indies. It soon

became known as California.

A romance novel of the early 1500s was the source of the name. In the book, California was an island rich in pearls and inhabited by "black women" living "in the fashion of Amazons." Their weapons were "all of gold...for in the whole island there was no metal but gold." Cortés's men had seen pearl oysters along the Baja coast and may well have named the new discovery optimistically after the fictional island. In 1535, Cortés attempted to establish a colony in Lower California. Its barren landscape and savage natives, who were unwilling to dive for oysters or do anything else for the white men, forced the colonists to abandon the "island."

In 1539, Cortés sent Francisco de Ulloa to continue exploring the area. Ulloa traveled far enough up the Gulf of California to realize Lower California was a peninsula. He also sailed down its east coast, rounded its tip, and sailed three-quarters of the way up its western coast until contrary winds forced him to turn back.

Although these expeditions expanded the map of the New World, they were financial disasters, costing Cortés 300,000 *castellanos* without returning a cent. Indomitable as ever, he prepared to fit out another fleet to find the real Cíbola. But Mendoza blocked his preparations, claiming for himself all right to explore north of New Spain. Cortés grew so frustrated by the viceroy's interference, in 1540 he sailed to Spain seeking redress from Charles V. Despite his past popularity, this time Cortés received no special treatment at the Spanish court. "Justice, proverbially slow in Spain, did not change her gait for Cortés," wrote Prescott. One year after Cortés's arrival, he had made no progress.

Restless and bored, in 1541, at the age of 56, he embarked as a volunteer in an offensive against the Moslems of Algiers. (The battle between Christians and Moslems had continued.) The campaign did not go well for the Christians, and their leaders decided to return home. Cortés, who had at one point offered to take the army and destroy the Moslem stronghold himself, was not consulted. "It was a marked indignity," writes Prescott, "but the courtiers, weary of service, were too much bent on an immediate return to Spain, to hazard the opposition of a man, who, when he had once planted his foot, was never known to raise it again, till he had accomplished his object." After his return to Spain, Cortés continued to petition the court for permission to explore.

Back in New Spain, with Cortés out of the way, Alvarado and Mendoza were the main contenders in the search for the Seven Cities. Alvarado had more experience as an explorer, but Mendoza had more power. After Alvarado and his new fleet left Honduras, they landed in the Mexican port of Guatulco to pick up supplies. Mendoza's soldiers blocked them from loading. Alvarado sailed farther north and again tried to replenish his fleet, but Mendoza again prevented it.

A meeting was arranged between the two and after heated bargaining they agreed to pool their resources and work together. Mendoza would receive half the profits from Alvarado's expeditions during the next 20 years, and Alvarado would get a fourth of any gains from Mendoza's during the same period.

When Cabrillo and the other private shipowners learned of the provisions of the agreement, they were furious. Alvarado had given half their potential profits to Mendoza without consulting them. Cabrillo appealed to Alvarado and received two valuable *encomiendas* near Santiago to make up for any losses he might sustain. But Cabrillo would receive no income from these properties; Alvarado's brother-in-law, Francisco de la Cueva, claimed title to them and embroiled Cabrillo and his heirs in a legal battle over their ownership for the next quarter century.

Mendoza and Alvarado had also agreed that they needed a sheltered homeport for their combined fleet, and in December they sent Cabrillo to seek it. Within two weeks he discovered a port, which became known as Navidad, in the province of Colima, and the ships of Mendoza and Alvarado were moved there.

The new partners' exploration plans called for Alvarado's fleet to be split and sent on two separate expeditions. One, led by Ruy López de Villalobos, was to head west across the Pacific. The other, commanded by Alvarado's nephew, Juan de Alvarado, would sail north and west up the Pacific coast.

Before these two expeditions could depart, Juan de Alvarado was called away to put down a nearby Indian revolt. Expedition assignments were juggled and new plans were being made when word reached Navidad that the Indian uprising had grown into a full-fledged war. Alvarado stripped his fleet of men and weapons and headed to the battlefront, while Cabrillo remained behind in Navidad in charge of the ships.

Against the advice of the local Spanish commanders, Alvarado charged into the heart of the battle, but the natives were protected by impregnable clifftops, and for the first time since he left Mexico 18 years earlier, Alvarado was defeated. During the retreat, a horse fell on him, crushing his chest. Mortally wounded, his "sins weighed more heavily upon him than bodily torture," reports Bancroft. Eager to unburden his "needful" soul, Alvarado anxiously called for a priest and spent his few remaining days confessing. He died on July 4, 1541 at the age of 56.

Alvarado's death left the army and fleet in disarray. Many of the soldiers returned to Guatemala, taking some of the ships with them. Mendoza took possession of the rest. Alvarado also left a long list of unpaid debts. Cabrillo and the others Alvarado owed filed claims against the estate, documenting the money due them. Unfortunately, the old *adelantado's* estate was too small to pay them, and no heirs

came forward to claim the estate, which would have entailed taking on Alvarado's debts as well. With no heirs, much of Alvarado's remaining property reverted to the crown, and many of the men he owed ended up in debtors' prison unable to pay their own bills.

Without a governor, Guatemala was in a state of confusion. The *cabildo*, or governing body, of Santiago sought a new leader to fill the void left by Alvarado. They were looking for someone with the Alvarado name or at least a strong connection to it, for fear of the old governor had kept the Indians in line. Bishop Marroquín favored Alvarado's nephew Juan, but Viceroy Mendoza ordered the *cabildo* to choose Francisco de la Cueva, Alvarado's brother-in-law. The colonists distrusted de la Cueva, whom Marroquín describes as having "no zeal for justice...and not much conscience." Many, including Cabrillo, had been cheated out of their *encomiendas* by him.

The search for a new governor gave Cabrillo a chance to get even with de la Cueva. In Navidad, the viceroy entrusted to Cabrillo the document ordering de la Cueva's selection as governor. Kelsey thinks Cabrillo purposely delayed delivering the viceroy's message to give the *cabildo's* members time to make their own decision. Eventually they elected Alvarado's widow, Beatriz, governor *pro tem.*, and de la Cueva lieutenant governor. De la Cueva was to administer the colony, but Beatriz would retain the right to grant *encomiendas*.

Bancroft implies that the loss of her husband affected Beatriz's sanity. Athough all Santiago grieved for the *adelantado*, "for however bad the man there are few who do not take pleasure in conventional mourning," Beatriz went to extremes. "She beat her face and tore her hair, weeping, screaming, and groaning in a very ecstasy of grief. For days she neither ate nor slept, refusing all consolation. She caused her house to be stained black, both inside and out, and draped it in deepest mourning. All efforts to appease her met with passionate outbursts...and she repulsed alike the appeals of friends and the religious consolation offered by the priests...."

Despite her grief, Beatriz accepted the position of governor. On September 9, 1541, she took the oath of office and signed a document naming de la Cueva lieutenant governor. After she wrote her name, she crossed it out and wrote "la sin ventura"—the unfortunate one.

Beatriz's intense mourning upset her neighbors because they thought it was unpious and they feared reprisals from God for her behavior. Some even blamed her for the disasters that followed. Writer Joan Lloyd tells that soon after Alvarado's demise, a number of mysterious fires destroyed buildings in Santiago, dogs trained to hunt Indians suddenly turned on the Spaniards' cattle, and a strange epidemic broke out.

Prescott reports that the day after Beatriz was selected governor, a severe tropical storm hit Guatemala. Pink lightning fractured the sky, and rain deluged the colony. In the wee hours of September 11, 1541, a powerful earthquake jolted the area, weakening the rain-soaked walls of the volcano overshadowing Santiago until they gave way and sent the crater's lake crashing down on the town. Tons of mud and boulders came with it, burying large portions of the city.

The governor's palace collapsed, killing Beatriz and her attendants. Legend says the flood washed Beatriz's body across the town square to the foot of the cathedral's altar. A fortune in gold amassed by Alvarado is said to be buried still under the mud. Most of the city's buildings were destroyed or badly damaged and hundreds of people died.

Cabrillo's house was destroyed, but his family was unharmed. Cabrillo was in Acajutla when the disaster struck, but he hurried to the capital soon afterward. As well as taking care of his family and other survivors, he wrote a concise report of the quake and its damage, which gives us much of the knowledge we have about the disaster. Written in the terse, pragmatic terms of a soldier, it uses phrases like "half a crossbow shot outside the city" to describe distances. He probably wrote the report as a letter to Juan de Alvarado, who sent a copy of it to Spain and one to a Mexico City printer. Published in late 1541, it is thought to be the first secular publication printed in the New World. (The published version varies slightly from the original; evidently censorship existed in 16th-century New Spain. Among other alterations, "Murio Robles the tailor died along with his lady friend," was changed to "Murio Robles the tailor died along with his *wife*.")

With most of the city destroyed and the governor killed, the residents of Santiago were again in turmoil. The *cabildo* solved the leadership problem by electing Bishop Marroquín and de la Cueva to serve as joint governors. Many locations were reviewed as sites for a new capital, but one only half a league from the old site was chosen. Known now as Antigua Guatemala, it was frighteningly close to the destroyed city, but it was also near the fields and farms of the colonists, which weren't destroyed by the earthquake. Many of the residents had been reduced to poverty by the disaster and preferred to risk another quake rather than give up what little they had left.

Cabrillo spent the remainder of 1541 moving his family to the new capital, but then he returned to Navidad. Viceroy Mendoza had commissioned him to lead a voyage of discovery.

The frontispiece of the published version of Cabrillo's earthquake report.

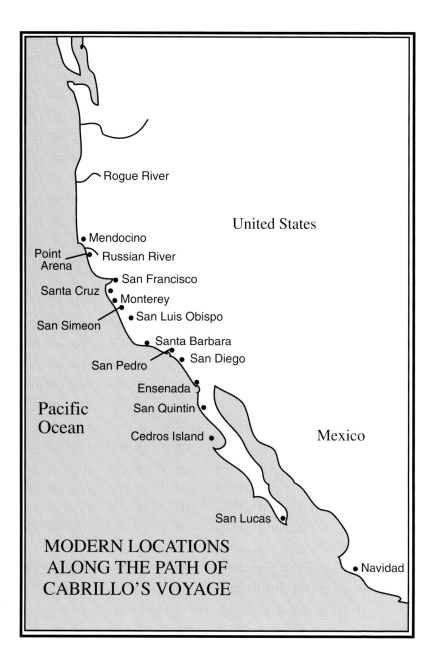

Rogue River

United States

Mendocino
Point
Arena
Russian River
San Francisco
Santa Cruz
Monterey
San Luis Obispo
San Simeon
Santa Barbara
San Pedro
San Diego
Ensenada
San Quintin
Pacific
Ocean
Cedros Island
Mexico
San Lucas
Navidad

MODERN LOCATIONS
ALONG THE PATH OF
CABRILLO'S VOYAGE

9

The Voyage

Oh! What hardships one endures
when discovering new lands....
　　　　　　　—Bernal Díaz del Castillo

After settling the Indian revolt that took Alvarado's life, Viceroy Mendoza was eager to get on with the expeditions he and Alvarado had planned. In early 1542, he asked Cabrillo to lead a group that would explore the Pacific coast north and west of New Spain, and Villalobos was finally to command an expedition west across the Pacific. Cabrillo would prepare the ships for both voyages.

Reassembling Alvarado's fleet was no small task. The ships and crew were scattered, and much of the equipment was missing. Some of the crew members had been killed by the quake, and others were not eager to go. Expeditions up the Pacific coast had been dismally unsuccessful, and the men's close call with death from the earthquake may have made them less eager to risk the dangers of the sea. Sailors of the Age of Exploration had a 50-50 chance of surviving to see their homes again. Most died from diseases of malnutrition, like scurvy, but storms, reefs, and hostile natives took their toll as well.

Cabrillo may also have questioned the wisdom of this expedition, but the earthquake and Alvarado's unpaid debts had reduced his wealth, and despite the failure of other voyages, treasure was surely there. If not Indian treasure, how far could China be? Besides, if the expedition was successful, Alvarado's estate would benefit and give Cabrillo a chance to recoup the money the late governor owed him.

Since there weren't enough willing volunteers, Cabrillo conscripted white men and Indians of both sexes. The official list of expedition members has been lost, but approximately 200 people were under Cabrillo's command.

Historians disagree on the number of ships he took. The original estimate was two, but Kelsey argues convincingly for three. The largest was Cabrillo's ship, the *San Salvador*, the 200-ton galleon also known as the *Juan Rodríguez*. Second in size was the *Victoria*, one of the 100-ton *naos*, or big-bellied ships, from Alvarado's fleet. Some historians think she originally was the *Alvar Núñez* whose name had been changed to that of the patron saint of sailors. The final major vessel, if there was one, was probably the *bergantín San Miguel*. Several small ship's boats were also taken. Used as utility vessels, they were either carried on board the bigger ships or towed behind them.

The *San Salvador* carried approximately 100 people. According to Kelsey, they included 4 officers, 25 or 30 crewmembers, 25 soldiers, a mixed group of about 24 Indians and black slaves, a few merchants and clerks, and at least one priest. The king required expeditions to include men of the cloth to spread Christianity among the Indians they encountered. The *Victoria* had 50 or 60 people assigned to her, and the *San Miguel* carried a crew of six or eight plus slaves and sailors manning the oars as punishment for misbehavior. Since a sailor's inattention to duty could send a ship crashing onto a reef, punishment for infractions was often brutal. Rowing was backbreaking labor, but far worse treatment greeted some offenders. One 17th-century English sea captain submitted his sailors to "ducking at the yards arme, [hauling] under the keel, [and binding] to the capsterne or maine-mast with a bucket of shot about [the] necke...."

The Indians in Cabrillo's crew were from Guatemala and Mexico. Some probably came from his *encomiendas*. Female natives kept the men "satisfied," and the male Indians worked as servants and laborers. One seaman on the expedition questioned their value, recommending, "Indians should not be taken on any voyage because they are not much use, and they eat the food."

Indians were at the bottom of the status ladder, but sailors weren't much higher. Generally illiterate, sailors were frequently shanghaied from the dregs of society; Columbus had collected many of his

crewmembers from prison. A sailor's life was hard and rewards few or nonexistent. Soldiers fared better, earning more pay and receiving better treatment. At the top of the status ladder were the officers. The captain was the highest in rank followed by the pilot, sailing master, and master's mate or chief boatswain.

Cabrillo's ships were well-supplied with food and materials to repair the vessels. Iron, rope, and caulking compounds were kept in the hold, as were cattle and horses. Food stores included wine, olive oil, hard bread, beans, saltmeat, and saltfish. Officers and wealthy passengers carried extra tidbits such as figs, raisins, prunes, and pots of jam to supplement this diet. Although at that time they were unaware of the value of the vitamin C in these luxury foods, people equipped with these treats fared better against scurvy than those without them.

Cabrillo's fleet had enough staple foods to last two years. Despite this apparent abundance, food often went bad, and crew members from many voyages of discovery told grim tales of life on board ship. One of Magellan's crew reported, "We ate only old biscuit reduced to powder, and full of grubs, and stinking from the dirt which rats had made on it...and we drank water that was yellow and stinking. We also ate the oxhides which were under the main yard..., the sawdust of wood, and rats." Great casks held the expedition's water. Often leaky, they were refilled by rain or fresh water from shore. When rain was absent and no creeks were to be found, desperate crew members were known to drink their own urine.

Although Cabrillo had been told to treat whatever Indians he encountered kindly (at least until colonies were established and *encomiendas* divided up), the ships were equipped with weapons. The *San Salvador* probably had two or three small cannons, and the soldiers carried swords, knives, crossbows, and arquebuses. Because gunpowder was difficult to keep dry at sea, and drying it required the risk of putting it near the cook-box, firearms were unpopular on ships.

Everyone expected the expedition to make money. Mendoza instructed Cabrillo to keep records of trading transactions, especially noting items that sold well. Cabrillo was also to keep his eyes open for potential sites for new settlements, and if he found an especially promising one, he was to set up a small colony.

Alvarado and Mendoza had intended both expeditions to reach the Orient. Cabrillo was to look for the Seven Cities or any other treasure he could find along the way, but his ultimate goal was Asia. People at that time had little idea of the true geography of the Pacific and greatly underestimated its size. They also believed the coast above colonized New Spain curved directly over to China. Maps did little to correct this impression. Rather than leave the unknown areas of the world blank, many cartographers added features famous from myths or biblical tales. They littered the Pacific with stepping-stone-like islands and bounded it on the north with a huge landmass linking Asia to New Spain.

Another feature that frequently appeared was the fictional Strait of Anián, known to the English as the Northwest Passage. This channel was believed to connect the Atlantic and Pacific oceans, providing Europe with a direct route to the Orient. Explorers spent centuries stubbornly seeking this elusive passage, believing God would not have created an obstacle between them and China without providing a passage through it. Although the name Strait of Anián does not appear in records until 1562, Cabrillo's orders included looking for a great river, which, if not this fabled strait, was probably another thought by a previous explorer to lead to the Spice Islands.

A stiff southeast wind was blowing at noon on Tuesday, June 27, 1542, as Cabrillo's three ships sailed out of Navidad harbor. What is known of their journey comes from a summary log thought to have been written by Juan León, a notary for the royal *audiencia* of Mexico. Cabrillo's original log was lost, but in those days it was not unusual for a government representative to write a summary of expeditions for official use. The summary was a brief, no-nonsense version of the log, incorporating information from interviews of crew members. Unfortunately, even León's summary has been lost, so we have to rely on a copy of it, probably made by Andrés de Urdaneta, a skilled, 16th-

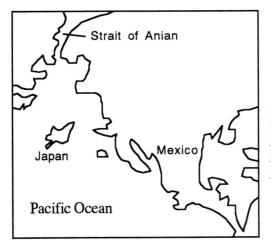

This is a simplified version of a 1566 map showing the fictional Strait of Anian and a misplaced Japan.

century navigator and cosmographer, who copied the information to help plan voyages of his own.

The style and content of the log change several times indicating different sources. The first part is attributed to Cabrillo, and the latter sections to one or two pilots and perhaps a priest. One of the pilots was undoubtedly Bartolomé Ferrer (also called Ferrelo), chief pilot of the expedition and commander of the *Victoria*. Because the crew list has been lost, the names of very few others on the voyage are known.

Cabrillo's entries list weather and sailing conditions, distances traveled, estimated latitudes, and the appearance of the shore with evaluations of its worth for anchorage and settlement. In the first 24 hours of the voyage, the southeast wind helped the three ships travel nearly 100 miles up the coast of New Spain. Then the wind turned against them, leaving them to wait four days before they could cross the Gulf of California. The log gives a clear picture of the tremendous impact weather had on sailing ships. Even with lateen sails, they could not travel up the Pacific Coast against a northwest wind—the prevailing wind of that coast. A member of a later Pacific coast expedition called it "the king and absolute master of this sea and coast." Throughout the voyage, members of Cabrillo's fleet would spend many days waiting for the wind to shift.

Daily life followed a routine—watches were changed, the helmsman relieved, and observations of the sun or North Star made at regular intervals. Time was kept with a half-hour sand glass, turned regularly by a ship's boy who made a mark on a board each time he turned the glass. The glass and board hung in the steerage, an enclosure in the sterncastle or below decks where charts were kept and the helmsman manned a heavy tiller or whipstaff to steer the ship. Through a hole in the ceiling of this room the captain of the watch, who was standing on the deck above, yelled down instructions and course changes to the helmsman.

The crew was divided in half. Half stood watch, while the others rested. Eight turns of the glass, or four hours, made a watch, and the afternoon watch was often dogged, or cut into two sections, so the same sailors didn't have the midnight to 4 a.m. watch each night. The section on watch was responsible for the ship, but all hands were called to duty during storms or other dangerous situations.

Historian Samuel E. Morison wrote, "In Spanish and Portuguese ships [routines] were observed with a quasi-religious ritual, which lent them a certain beauty and served to remind the seamen every half-hour of the day and night that their ship depended for safety not only on her staunchness and their own skill, but on the grace of God." Each turning of the glass was accompanied by a short prayer, and the ship's boy greeted the morning watch with sentiment along the lines of: "God give us good days, good voyage, good passage to the ship, sir Captain and Master and good company, amen; so let there be a good voyage."

The first chores of the day included scrubbing the deck with saltwater. The new helmsman received his course from the captain of the previous watch, and lookouts were posted fore and aft. The retiring watch captain recorded the events of his watch in the log. The ship's captain received his breakfast and a bucket of sea water for washing from his servant, and then went on deck to join in morning prayers, which he or the ship's priest led. Other regular duties included pumping the bilge (bottom of the hold) of water that had leaked in during the night, keeping the decks clear, setting and trimming sails, and maintaining and repairing gear. Before the night watch was set, the captain or priest led evening prayer, including the ship's boy's request, "God give us a good night and good sailing; may the ship make a good passage, Sir Captain and Master and good company."

On July 2, the winds changed, allowing Cabrillo's ships to cross the Gulf of California. The next day they anchored off the tip of Lower California. Two days later, they traveled to a nearby cove known as

A sounding lead.

San Lucas, which had good anchorage and fresh water. Anchorages were evaluated with the use of a "lead," a heavy lead weight tied to the end of a rope. Leads had a socket filled with sticky tallow that picked up samples of the bottom of a potential anchoring site. The length of rope used to reach the bottom indicated the depth of water, and the bottom samples gave an idea of how well the anchor would hold. At San Lucas the expedition members rested and replenished their wood and water supply.

Cabrillo was fortunate to have a copy of a map prepared in 1541 by Domingo del Castillo. Remarkably accurate, it showed the west coast of New Spain and Lower California as far north as Cabo del Engaño (present-day Point Baja)—the northernmost point reached by Ulloa three years earlier. He was also lucky to have onboard at least one person who had traveled to Lower California with previous expeditions. This person was invaluable during the first part of the voyage, for good seamen had excellent memories for where water, wood, and food could be found.

On July 8, the ships left San Lucas, but sailed only a short distance before unfavorable winds again forced them to anchor off the coast. At this particular place, it was impossible to go ashore because there wasn't any landing. Even if there had been, fear of Indian attack would have kept the voyagers on board. Except for brief forays ashore, it was rare for expedition members to leave the ship.

Kelsey believes all Cabrillo's ships were fully decked, which means even the small *San Miguel*, if it made the journey, probably had an enclosed area to protect cargo and provide shelter from hot sun and storms. The headroom below deck was generally five feet or less on ships of that era, and the conditions were so unpleasant that exposure to storms might have been preferable. Although the ships were impressively watertight if their caulking was maintained, there was always some leakage. This water along with waste from cattle, horses, rats, and humans, various food scraps, and other unappealing items collected among the ballast in the bilge. Despite regular pumping, this "soup" created such "foul stinkes" and "pestilential funkes" as to make the hold nearly intolerable. One Spaniard thought the "fumes" when combined with the "heate of men couched close and neare together in a narrowe place," exploded to cause the glow of static electricity seen on masts during storms and known as St. Elmo's fire.

Sailors, soldiers, and slaves slept wrapped in blankets or sail scraps wherever they could find a place to brace themselves against the rolling of the ship. The captain and a few other people of rank had bunks in the sterncastle. The crew's few possessions were generally lashed to the bulwarks in trunks below decks.

The crew provided their own attire, and no provisions were made for foul-weather gear. Morison reports that 16th-century notions of hygiene required them to wear wool from neck to foot whatever the temperature. Since the sailors only owned one set of clothing and wore it day and night, cleanliness was difficult, if not impossible, to maintain. Morison says Spanish and Portuguese sailors were a "cleanly lot." At the end of the day they washed themselves in a bucket of salt water and went ashore, when it was safe, to launder their clothes in fresh water. The same can't be said for English sailors. One 17th-century British officer recommended the government provide seamen with a second set of clothes "for the preservation of health and as to avoid nasty beastliness to which many of the men are subject by continual wearing of one suit of clothes."

On August 20, 1542, Cabrillo passed Cabo del Engaño. The wind had kept Ulloa from rounding this point, but Cabrillo had no trouble. From that point on, the expedition was in uncharted waters.

Knowing he was now the first European to explore these lands, Cabrillo began a regular process of naming the various landmarks they passed and claiming them for the king. Taking possession was a serious act during the Age of Discovery, and each country developed its own conventions to symbolize its claim. Portuguese explorers set up inscribed stone pillars, and Elizabethan Englishmen set up a royal standard or made a pile of stones. The Spanish usually erected a cross

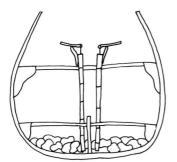

Despite bilge pumps, the holds of sailing ships filled with water and a variety of noxious wastes.

and performed several actions representing their control over the land. Names were chosen that described a special feature of the new acquisition or honored the saint on whose feast day it was found. Successive Spanish explorers claimed the same land over and over to reinforce their ownership.

During a formal ceremony on August 22, Cabrillo made his first act of possession. "In the name of His Majesty and in the illustrious name of Don Antonio Mendoza," he claimed the port now known as San Quintín, naming it Posesión. Placing his hand on his sword, he vowed to defend it against all who contradicted the claim, and then he cut three slashes into a tree, moved some stones from one place to another, and poured water from the sea onto the land.

Posesión was backed with "high and rolling mountains" and had a beach where ships could easily be drawn ashore for repairs. The expedition stayed there for five days, probably taking time to repair the leaking *San Miguel*.

While there, they made their first contact with Indians. One day they came upon two women and a boy who were obviously afraid of the strange-looking white men. Gifts of trinkets and clothing encouraged a larger group of natives to visit later. According to the log, they were a "tall and healthy people." Some of the natives had decorated their bodies with a white "ointment" to resemble Spanish pantaloons and short jackets. Through sign language, they told of having seen more Spaniards five days' journey inland. This was the first of many times Cabrillo would hear this story. It probably referred to men from

Coronado's party who had reached the Colorado River months earlier. The Indians living along the coast of northern Baja California and present-day southern California lived in independent villages linked to each other and far-reaching trade routes by well-worn trails. News of anything as remarkable as white men probably traveled quickly along these paths. Cabrillo gave the Indians a letter to carry to the other Spaniards and then set sail on August 27.

Throughout the voyage, latitudes, compass directions, and distances were determined and included in the log. Latitudes were established by the use of a cross-staff or astrolabe. These instruments required the user to align its sights with the horizon and either the sun or North Star. The angle between the two was read off a scale of degrees on the instrument. The angle was then translated into a latitude, or north-south location, using tables in a book of declination. Few mariners had the math ability or patience to do this accurately, and it was impossible to get a precise reading on a pitching ship. Latitudes determined on land were more accurate.

Longitude, the east-west location of a point, requires an accurate timepiece to determine. The sand glass wasn't accurate enough; rough seas and the irregular attention of the boys in charge of turning the glass caused too many errors. Chronometers wouldn't be invented for centuries, so none of the explorers of Cabrillo's era could figure longitude.

Although Cabrillo was a reasonably good navigator, his latitudes were off by between 1 and 2 degrees (60 and 120 miles). Compasses were quite precise at that time, but Cabrillo's was corrected to work in Seville, not the magnetic declination of the California coast. His compass readings erred by between 15 and 20 degrees. Distances traveled at that time were measured by guessing the ship's speed. Mariners familiar with their vessel grew very good at estimating its speed. Sometimes they got help by throwing a piece of wood from the bow and seeing how long it took to travel the distance of the hull. Cabrillo's estimates of distance were very good. However, his inconsistent errors in direction and latitude make it impossible for us to know exactly where he was throughout his voyage.

In mid-September, the barren landscape of the southern portion of Lower California gave way to "another sort of country....It is red earth

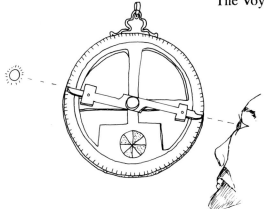

and better looking." On the 17th, Cabrillo took possession of San Mateo, now known as Ensenada, Mexico, which he described as having "good land with large savannas and grass like that in Spain."

Near the end of September, expedition members saw the first of many "great smokes"—dense clouds of smoke from fires set by natives. The Kumeyaay, who inhabited the area from Ensenada to just south of present-day Oceanside, California, burned parts of their territory each fall after harvesting grass seeds and acorns. This practice enriched the soil and improved the following year's crop. Game animals—rabbits, deer, birds, and rodents—also benefitted from the improved browse, giving the Kumeyaay a rich natural larder.

On September 28, the three ships entered a "port enclosed and very good," where they stayed for six days to avoid the first major storm of the season. This was San Diego Bay, which Cabrillo called San Miguel. Historians think Cabrillo anchored off Ballast Point, which is now a small finger of land near the mouth of the bay. The anchorage was so sheltered, "they felt nothing" from the storm.

The Kumeyaay Cabrillo encountered in San Diego were obviously frightened of the Spaniards. They weren't sure if the bearded, armored men were human, animal, or insect. (Two centuries later the Spaniards' cruel treatment would make the Kumeyaay decide the intruders were evil witches.) Despite gifts of trinkets and clothes, several Indians attacked and wounded three sailors who had gone ashore to fish. Cabrillo showed remarkable restraint by not returning their attack. Through more gifts, he encouraged the Indians to visit peaceably. The natives showed through signs that "inland there

walked men like the Spaniards, bearded and dressed and armed like the ones on the ships, and they showed that they had [crossbows], and made gestures with their right arm as if they were spearing. They went running as if they were on a horse, and showed they killed many of the Indian natives, and for that reason they were afraid."

The fleet left San Diego on October 3, passing the islands of Santa Catalina and San Clemente, and entering the bay of San Pedro. They named it Bay of Smokes for the dense clouds caused by numerous Indian grass fires.

On October 10 they arrived at an Indian town where the "houses were large like those of New Spain." The beach was lined with well-built canoes, which soon filled with Indians paddling out to see the strange ships. Unlike the Kumeyaay, these people were confident and curious. They were the Chumash, members of a successful and well-developed culture that had been established in the area for thousands of years. Their territory stretched from Malibu to San Luis Obispo and included the Channel Islands off the California coast. They too told of other white men inland, but rather than being intimidated, they shared food with the Spaniards and made them welcome. Cabrillo named this village, located near today's Mugu Lagoon, Pueblo de las Canoas.

For the next few weeks he sailed along the Santa Barbara coast and investigated the Channel Islands. Four of the islands—San Miguel, Santa Rosa, Santa Cruz, and Anacapa—are near Santa Barbara. The rest—San Clemente, Santa Catalina, San Nicolas, and Santa Barbara Island—had already been passed. The log hopelessly confuses the islands. It includes testimony from several members of the expedition and each of them gives different names to the islands. Even without this problem, Cabrillo himself created a muddle by giving the same name to many of the islands and multiple names to a few. He called some the San Lucas group and others the "other islands of San Lucas." Nearly every one was called Posesión at one time or another, and one specific island was known variously as San Miguel, Posesión, Juan Rodríguez, and Cápitana. Historians disagree on which island is which.

While exploring the islands, Cabrillo learned from the Chumash about a large river up the coast to the north. Perhaps hoping it was a shortcut to the Spice Islands, Cabrillo headed north on November 6 to look for it. On the night of November 11, near present-day San Simeon, a severe storm hit the three ships. The log reports, "The weather from the south-southeast worsened so much with rain in the southwest, and darkness, that they could not have a palm of sail, and were forced to run with a close-reefed [shortened] piece of sail on the foremast, with much work all night, and on Sunday the weather grew so much worse that that day and night were ruined, and it continued until Monday at midday. The storm was as violent as any could be in Spain, and on Saturday night the ships lost sight of each other." Because survival during a voyage frequently depended on crews helping each other out, losing sight of a companion vessel was terrifying.

Storms also brought fear. Against powerful winds, sailors could only pray and decrease the amount of sail, hoping to reduce how much the wind tossed them around. During storms Christopher Columbus read the Bible aloud and reported both men and waves were calmed when he read Christ's words to his disciples, "Fear not, it is I." English seamen sang "Helpe Lord for good and godly men," and Cabrillo's men on the *San Salvador* promised to make a pilgrimage to the Virgin's shrine if she would but spare them from the deep. The crew of the *Victoria* undoubtedly uttered their own prayers as they desperately tried to keep their ship together. Despite their efforts, the *Victoria* lost her deck cargo and sustained major damage.

The storm forced the *San Salvador* out to sea, but when it abated, the ship turned back to the coast. Despite the loss of companion ships, Cabrillo ordered the crew to continue north. Along the way they named a point they encountered Cabo de Pinos for its evergreen-covered hills. Whether it was north or south of San Francisco is debatable, but the *San Salvador* clearly missed the opening to that large bay. Kelsey believes Cabrillo continued north to the mouth of the Russian River, and then, disappointed that he hadn't found the great river he was seeking, turned south to look for his companions. On the 15th, they found the *Victoria* and *San Miguel* at anchor near Santa Cruz. The crews were worn out and half frozen.

The world's climate was colder then. A cool-moist cycle had begun during the late 1300s and wouldn't change to today's warm-dry cycle until the mid-1800s. The rich green savannas Cabrillo had seen at Ensenada and San Diego were a result of this trend (now he'd see only dry chaparral), and so were the cold winds and snow-covered shores of central California that chilled his crew.

While the *Victoria's* sailors fixed their leaky vessel, Cabrillo explored Monterey Bay, continuing to look for a large river. When none was found, all three ships headed south. The steep, frozen cliffs of Big Sur offered no landing, so it wasn't until November 23, when the ships were back at the Channel Islands that the crew found respite. The sailors of the *San Miguel* hauled their ship on shore to fix the leaks, which had become so bad the crew feared their vessel would sink.

Historians disagree about where the fleet spent the majority of that winter. Storms forced them to change anchorage frequently, and the confusion of island names in the log makes it impossible to follow their travels. The island called Capitana seemed to offer the best shelter. Some historians think Capitana was San Miguel, the westernmost island of the chain near Santa Barbara. Anthropologist Heizer thought San Miguel's eastern neighbor, Santa Rosa Island, was Capitana, while Kelsey thinks it was Santa Catalina, one of the islands to the south of the main Channel Island group.

Whichever island it was, its native residents soon grew tired of the Spaniards. The Spaniards had amiable relationships with some of the

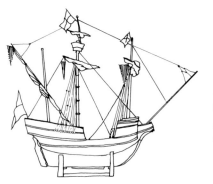

This model of the San Salvador *is on display at Cabrillo National Monument in San Diego, California.*

Chumash, but the island Chumash were the poorest and most aggressive and let the Spaniards know they had worn out their welcome by starting a running battle with them. During one of these skirmishes, Cabrillo was injured.

Several of his men had been attacked while they were on shore getting water, and Cabrillo had assembled a rescue party to save them. Francisco de Vargas, who was a member of the party, reported that they rowed to the island and when Cabrillo "began to jump out of the boat, one foot struck a rocky ledge, and he splintered a shinbone." Cabrillo refused to return to the ship before all his men were safe.

Some sources disagree with Vargas and say Cabrillo injured a shoulder or arm, and the summary log implies the injury occurred before the ships sailed north from the Channel Islands. Whatever Cabrillo damaged and whenever he did it, the wound festered and became gangrenous in the last days of December. Realizing he was going to die, Cabrillo passed his command to chief pilot Ferrer and ordered him to carry out the expedition's commission. Cabrillo tried to finish writing his part of the log but was too weak to cover the voyage north of the islands. On January 3, 1543, he died. His men buried him on the island they called Capitana.

Ferrer took his new responsibility seriously. Several times he headed out to sea to continue the expedition, but each time winds forced him back. Finally, on February 14, the small fleet met favorable winds, and on the 25th, they passed the northernmost point of the expedition's previous journey. Strong winds sent them running farther north past shoreline that was "rugged and without shelter" and showed no sign of Indians.

On the 26th, they passed Pt. Arena, which they called Cabo de

Fortunas, and they continued to a point they thought was 43 or 44 degrees of latitude. Authorities don't agree on how far north Ferrer really went. Some say as far as the present Washington state border, while others say no farther than Mendocino in California. Kelsey believes he reached the Rogue River in present-day Oregon. However far it was, the ships were pushed there by another storm. On March 1, "at dawn the wind shifted to the southwest with much fury, and the seas came from every direction, and they broke over the ships...[which] surely would not have escaped sinking if God had not come to their assistance. It was impossible to lay to, therefore they ran with the bow to the northeast before the wind toward the land. Taking themselves for lost, they commended themselves to Our Lady of Guadalupe, and made offerings."

Their prayers were answered by a shift in wind which allowed them to turn south toward the sheltering Channel Islands. The storm damaged their supplies, and the log reports people "suffered for food." They were also exhausted, and many were ill after months of exposure and limited diets.

On the night of March 5, they arrived at the Channel Islands, but a storm prevented them from anchoring. The wind was so fierce it separated the ships, and once again each crew feared the "ocean had devoured" the others.

When the weather allowed, each vessel headed south on its own. It would be weeks before they met again and the crews knew they were all safe. The *San Salvador* stopped at Pueblo de las Canoas and "took on" four Indians the crew intended to teach Spanish. They were to serve as interpreters on later voyages. The Spaniards picked up two more natives at San Diego on March 11. Finally, on March 26, all three ships were reunited at Cedros Island in Lower California, and the crews shared tales of their adventures. One ship had been grounded on a sand bar but was set free by "Our Lady" after "the sailors had promised to go to their churches naked...."

The three battered ships and their ailing crews headed home. "They had no provisions," the log tells us, "to enable them to return to carry on further discoveries along the coast." They reached Navidad on April 14, 1543, less than 10 months after they left.

Mendoza was bitterly disappointed by the results of this and the

Villalobos expedition. Neither had met its goals and the leaders of both had died during the voyages. Mendoza refitted Cabrillo's ships and sent them and their crews on a trading voyage to Peru. None of the ships returned, and few of the crewmembers survived to come back to Navidad.

Antonio de Remesal, an early 17th-century Dominican scholar, sums up the fate of the fleet built by Juan Rodríguez Cabrillo for Pedro de Alvarado: "The entire fleet perished," he wrote, "some eaten by shipworms, others scattered to different ports in disorder, because the *adelantado* had died." Not everyone would agree with Remesal that the armada failed because of Alvarado's death, but few would argue with the bleakness of his assessment. Such was the fate of the grand fleet built by Cabrillo.

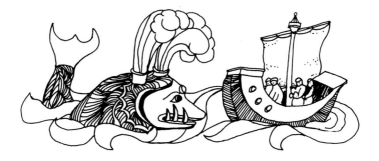

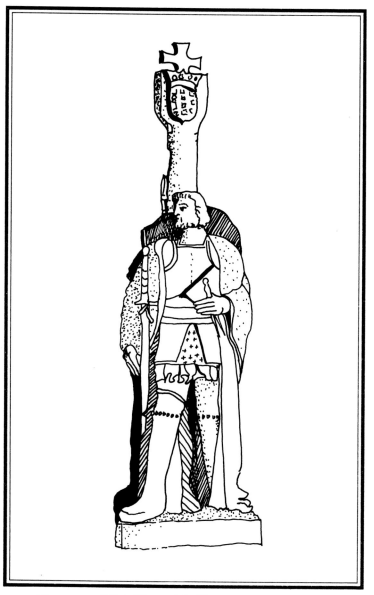

The statue of Cabrillo at Cabrillo National Monument.

10

End of an Era

Although ambition and love of action are common to all, as to the advantages that each may gain, there are great inequities of fortune, the result not of conduct, but only accident....

—John Upton Terrell, biographer of Alvar Núñez Cabeza de Vaca

After word of Cabrillo's death reached Guatemala, Francisco de la Cueva claimed more of Cabrillo's *encomiendas*, and a religious order took over Cobán. Without the income from these properties, Cabrillo's family was reduced to poverty. His widow remarried (Juan de Aguilar, another resident of Santiago), but she and Cabrillo's oldest son would spend the rest of their lives involved in lawsuits trying to recoup Cabrillo's wealth. It wasn't until 1617, when Cabrillo's grandson Jeronimo Cabrillo de Aldana petitioned for restitution of his grandfather's property that the case was settled. And even then the resolution was far from satisfying. It gave the Cabrillo family a stipulated amount of income from an *encomienda*, but since no *encomiendas* were available, they were to receive the money only after one became vacant.

The documents created in these years of litigation tell much of what we know about Cabrillo. They contain testimony from many of his contemporaries who were called to document Cabrillo's service to Spain and establish the family's right to the rewards due him.

Fellow conquistador Bernal Díaz del Castillo testified, "I knew [Juan Rodríguez Cabrillo] in New Spain and I declare that he...served

in the conquest and capture of the City of Mexico and vicinity. I saw him serve always with the diligence such conquests demand...he was a very capable man."

Francisco de Vargas, one of the crew members on Cabrillo's final expedition, testified about Cabrillo's accomplishments during the voyage. He finished his statement by saying, "If Cabrillo had not died he would have discovered the great country of spices and the Moluccas, which they were on their way to find, and perhaps would have gone even further if there was promise of anything there to discover, as he had that intention and the willingness to outdo all previous captains and discoverers."

Despite these testimonials and others given by those who knew him, the Spanish government never fully reinstated Cabrillo's possessions. His widow and sons were victims not only of de la Cueva's greed, but also of a dramatic change in the overall interests and direction of Spain's New World colonies. Ironically, Cabrillo contributed to this change. His expedition and that of Coronado made it clear no more gold-rich civilizations were to be found in the land north and west of New Spain. Hernando De Soto had proven the same thing for the territory north and east of New Spain. Between 1539 and 1542, he had explored from Florida to Kansas and found no sign of treasure. As a result of these expeditions, the energy and funds of the crown and the New World colonists were redirected to develop the land and resources they already had.

Men like Cortés and Alvarado, whose phenomenal courage, lightning tactics, and unquenchable thirst for risk and adventure had won the New World, were being replaced by lawyers, merchants, settlers, and priests—people who lived at a slower pace and whose accomplishments were more stable and long-lasting.

Laws from Spain reflected the change. Initially, the New World had offered the conquistadors opportunities for financial gain neither Spain or Portugal could match, and that was one of the reasons they had crossed the Atlantic. Having risked their lives in the conquests of Mexico and Central America, they felt entitled to their *encomiendas* and expected to keep them within their families and pass them from generation to generation. In 1542 and 1543, however, Charles V rescinded previous rulings granting rights of inheritance through at least the conquistadors' grandchildren, and he also ordered an end to native slave labor. Viceroy Mendoza, realizing the conquistadors would not tolerate the laws and knowing New Spain's economy depended on Indian labor, refused to enforce them.

Twenty years later, however, Charles's successor, Philip II, ordered *encomiendas* to revert to the crown after the death of the original owners' children. The colonists were outraged, but most of the original conquistadors were dead, and their children, raised in more refined circumstances than their fathers, were neither ruthless enough nor well enough organized to resist the government. A small, half-hearted rebellion formed around Cortés's son, Don Martín Cortés, but it was quickly quashed by the beheading of two of its members. Under the new system, *encomiendas* and government positions were sold to the highest bidder or given to those with the strongest political connections. For all intents and purposes, the conquest society was over by the middle of the 1540s.

Alvarado, Cabrillo, and many of their companions were dead by that time. Cortés, who in so many ways personified the conquest, died in Spain in 1547, at the age of 63. He had spent the last eight years of his life waiting in vain for Charles V to give him permission to continue searching for a route to the Orient. At one time during this frustrating period, the proud old conqueror reportedly thrust his way through the royal guards and confronted the king, who had refused to see him. Charles disdainfully inquired who he was, and Cortés supposedly answered, "I'm the man who conquered more provinces for you than you had cities when you took the throne."

Cortés coat of arms.

Cortés could have spent his last years in luxury on his estate in Oaxaca, but like so many conquistadors, he couldn't settle down. Prescott explains, "Dangers and difficulties...seemed to have a charm in his eyes." At a time when the average life expectancy was 30 years, Cortés in his 60s was planning more voyages of discovery. He wrote, "The lust for glory extends beyond this mortal life and taking a whole world will hardly satisfy it, much less one or two kingdoms."

Cortés died frustrated and neglected, but in his lifetime he had been gloriously honored and in history he is revered as a brilliant tactician and extraordinary leader. Fate was less kind to most of his subordinates, particularly Cabrillo. Besides the financial setbacks suffered by his family, his reputation was treated shabbily. His voyage, for which he gave his life, was considered a failure in its time because it found neither gold nor a route to the Orient.

In fact, it was no small accomplishment, adding approximately 800 miles of coastline to the map of the known world and requiring no less courage or skill as a seaman and leader than the voyages of Columbus. After reviewing Cabrillo's exploits, historian and skilled sailor Morison wrote admiringly, "There can be no doubt of [Cabrillo's] ability at sea." And a late 18th-century naval officer who had traversed the same course as Cabrillo wrote, "Those who know the coast which Cabrillo discovered and explored, the kind of vessels in which he undertook the expedition, the rigorous season during which he pursued his voyage in those intemperate climes, and the state of the science of navigation at that period, cannot help admiring a courage and intrepidity which...cannot be appreciated in our day...."

Another blow dealt to Cabrillo's reputation was the altering of the names he so diligently gave his discoveries. Mysteriously, the information collected during his expedition didn't reach Europe or appear on maps for several decades after his voyage. When it did, the names were soon changed. Spain had lost interest in California after Cabrillo's voyage. A would-be explorer of the late 16th century received this reply when seeking permission to explore farther up the Pacific coast—"Enough land has been discovered for His Majesty." However, a personality conflict between the viceroy of New Spain and an irritating merchant sent one more Spanish expedition up the California coast.

At the end of the 16th century, Juan Sebastián Vizcaíno, an unscrupulous merchant, became interested in harvesting pearls in the Gulf of California. The viceroy of New Spain so despised Vizcaíno that to get him out of his territory, he sent him on an expedition. Vizcaíno was to find new ports for ships involved in the lucrative Philippine trade Spain had started in 1565.

To make sure Vizcaíno followed orders, the viceroy sent two committees to guide him. He was to make no decisions without consulting them, and under no circumstances was he to change the names Cabrillo had given to coastal landmarks. The expedition left New Spain in 1602, and despite his committees, Vizcaíno managed to rename nearly all Cabrillo's discoveries, claiming Cabrillo's descriptions were too vague. Consequently, only a few of Cabrillo's names survive, Cape San Martín, Point Mugu, and Morro Rock in Morro Bay among them, but the majority of names used now for locations along the coast of Lower and Upper California—such as San Diego, Monterey, and Mendocino—are Vizcaíno's.

If Cabrillo had discovered gold or a route to the Orient, the history of California would be quite different, and we would probably know more about him. As it was, the natives of southern California were spared Spanish exploitation for another 200 years (it wasn't until the mid-1700s, when Russians began establishing colonies along the northern California coast, that Spain felt her sovereignty threatened enough to begin colonizing California herself) and Cabrillo remains relatively veiled by time. Coming so soon after the great discoveries of Tenochtitlán and the Inca empire, Cabrillo's expedition appears insignificant—anticlimactic in fact—in the annals of history, and Cabrillo himself is overshadowed by his flamboyant commanders, Cortés and Alvarado.

Cabrillo's life nearly spanned Spain's spectacular age of conquest in the New World—a brief 50-year period when the vast continents of North and South America went from being completely unknown to Europeans, to being nearly circumnavigated by them. In that same short time, those serving under the Spanish flag managed to conquer the continents' largest and most powerful civilizations and establish viable colonies of their own. Their reprehensible tactics can't be justified. But without them, the flood of precious metals that reached Europe from the New World would not have been available to further the great economic, intellectual, and scientific growth taking place there.

The conquistadors were ruthless soldiers of fortune, but they were also remarkable men, possessing uncommon courage, resilience, and faith. They belonged to a special breed of humanity that dominates brief times in history when their unique talents are in demand. Even in death they surprise us. The wills of both Cortés and Alvarado reveal unexpected concerns about the exploitation of natives. Alvarado's concerns are based, not surprisingly, on self-interest, but they still show an amazing awareness of moral issues his behavior didn't reveal. His will ordered his natives freed after they produced enough gold to pay his debts. His only request of them after that was to support two chaplaincies devoted to saying daily masses for his soul and that of his wife.

Cortés ended his will with this remarkable statement, "It has long been a question, whether one can conscientiously hold property in Indian slaves. Since this point has not yet been determined, I enjoin it on my son Martín and his heirs, that they spare no pains to come to an exact knowledge of the truth; as a matter which deeply concerns the conscience of each of them, no less than mine."

In his eighties, Bernal Díaz del Castillo, who served with Cabrillo in the army of Cortés and who was a neighbor of his in Santiago, wrote an extraordinary history of the conquest of Mexico. Impoverished, as Cabrillo's family had been, when the conquistadors fell from favor, he wrote, "I am now an old man..., and I have lost my sight and hearing, and, as luck would have it, I have gained nothing of value to leave to my children and descendants but this my true story, and they will presently find out what a wonderful story it is."

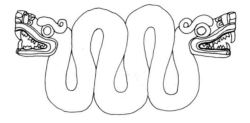

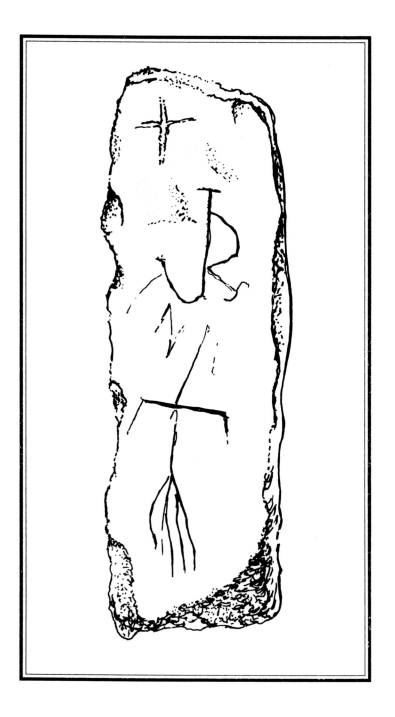

Epilogue

The stone Philip Jones found in 1901 lay forgotten for more than 70 years before catching Robert Heizer's attention. In the process of checking out whether it might be Cabrillo's gravemarker, Heizer considered a number of things. Could its inscription—a cross, human stick figure, and the letters *JR*—have been faked by Jones, he wondered? Jones's apparent disinterest in the artifact made it unlikely.

Although some people questioned why Cabrillo's gravemarker would contain only the letters *JR*, Heizer knew Cabrillo was commonly known as Juan Rodríguez to his contemporaries.

Heizer sent photos of the stone to three authorities on Spanish life during the 1500s. Each replied that the cross and initials were consistent with the content of gravemarkers of Cabrillo's era, but the human stick figure bothered them. It bothered Heizer too. Natives had carved similar ones on other stones on the Channel Islands. So Heizer hypothesized they probably carved this one too either before or after the Spaniards placed the stone on Cabrillo's grave.

The location where the stone was found—Santa Rosa Island—did not match the commonly accepted site of Cabrillo's burial—San Miguel Island. Heizer attributed this inequity to the confusion in the voyage log over the names of the Channel Islands. After reviewing the log for himself, he believed Santa Rosa could have been the island the Spaniards called Capitana and the burial site of Cabrillo.

By the end of his investigation, Heizer felt comfortable enough with his research to resolve the question of the stone's identity, at least for himself. "I do believe," he wrote, "that it is highly probable that we have here the stone which was carved in 1543 and set over the grave of Cabrillo."

Highly probable, perhaps, but not certain. The facts of Cabrillo's death, after all these years, remain just as elusive as many of the facts of his life. He was, and still is, a man of mystery.

Bibliography

Arnold, Jim. "Introduction to the Crossbow." Cabrillo National Monument. Unpub. paper.

Bancroft, Hubert Howe. *History of Central America*. The Works of Hubert Howe Bancroft, vol. VI. San Francisco: A.L. Bancroft, 1883.

————. *The North Mexican States*. History of the Pacific States of North America, vol. X. San Francisco: A.L. Bancroft, 1883.

Branco, F. Castelo. *Cabrillo's Nationality*. Lisbon: Academia de Marinha, 1987.

Brown, Joseph E. *Cabrillo National Monument*. San Diego: Cabrillo Historical Assn., 1981.

Carrico, Richard L. "Before the Strangers: American Indians in San Diego at the Dawn of Conquest." In *The Impact of European Exploration and Settlement on Local Native Americans*. San Diego: Cabrillo Historical Assn., 1986.

Castlereagh, Duncan. *The Great Age of Exploration*. Encyclopedia of Discovery and Exploration, vol. 3. London: Aldus Book, 1971.

Chatterton, E. Keble. *Sailing Ships*. Philadelphia: J.B. Lippincott, 1909.

Cheyney, Edward P. *European Background of American History: 1300-1600*. New York: Frederick Unger Publishing, 1904.

Connell, Evan S. *A Long Desire*. San Francisco: North Point Press, 1988.

Cumming, W.P. and R. A. Skelton. *The Discovery of North America*. New York: American Heritage Press, 1971

Díaz del Castillo, Bernal. *The Discovery and Conquest of Mexico*, 1517-1521. A.P. Maudslay, trans. New York: Farrar, Straus and Cudahy, 1956.

Freitas, William J. "Weapons of the Age of Navigation." In *16th Century Explorers*. San Diego: Cabrillo Historical Assn., 1975.

Fuentes, Patricia de, ed. and trans. *The Conquistadors*. New York: Orion Press, 1963.

Gardiner, C. Harvey. *Naval Power in the Conquest of Mexico*. New York: Greenwood Press, 1956.

Hale, John R. *Age of Exploration*. New York: *Time*, 1966.

Heizer, Robert F. *California's Oldest Relic?* Berkeley, CA: Robert H. Lowie Museum of Anthropology, University of California, 1972.

Horderne, Nicholas. *God, Gold and Glory*. Encyclopedia of Discovery and Exploration, vol. 4. London: Aldus Book, 1971.

Humble, Richard. *The Explorers*. The Seafarers. Alexandria, VA: Time-Life Books, 1979.

Innes, Hammond. *The Conquistadors*. New York: Alfred A. Knopf, 1969.

Jacobs, W.J. *Hernando Cortés*. New York: Franklin Watts, 1974.

Kelsey, Harry. *Juan Rodríguez Cabrillo*. San Marino, CA: Huntington Library, 1986.

Kemp, Peter, ed. *The Oxford Companion to Ships and the Sea*. London: Oxford University Press, 1976.

Lethbridge, T.C. "Shipbuilding." In *The Mediterranean Civilizations and the Middle Ages*. A History of Technology, vol. II. New York: Oxford University Press, 1957.

Lloyd, Joan. *Land of the Mayas*. London: Robert Hale, 1963.

McCall, Lynne and Rosalind Perry, coords. *California's Chumash Indians*. San Luis Obispo, CA: EZ Nature Books, 1988.

Meyer, Michael C. and William L. Sherman. *The Course of Mexican History*. New York: Oxford University Press, 1979.

Morison, Samuel E. *The European Discovery of America: The Northern Voyages, A.D. 500-1600*. New York: Oxford University Press, 1971.

————. *The European Discovery of America: The Southern Voyages, A.D. 1492-1616*. New York: Oxford University Press, 1974.

Naish, G.P.B. "Ships and Shipbuilding." In *From the Renaissance to the Industrial Revolution*. A History of Technology, vol. II. New York: Oxford University Press, 1957.

Napier, William. *Lands of Spice and Treasure*. Encyclopedia of Discovery and Exploration, vol. 5. London: Aldus Book, 1971.

Payne-Gallwey, Ralph. *The Crossbow*. New York: Bramhall House, 1958.

Prescott, William H. *History of the Conquest of Mexico, and History of the Conquest of Peru*. New York: Modern Library, 1843.

Reupsch, Carl F., ed. *The Cabrillo Era and His Voyage of Discovery*. San Diego: Cabrillo Historical Assn., 1982.

Shipek, Florence C. "The Impact of Europeans upon Kumeyaay Culture." In *The Impact of European Exploration and Settlement on Local Native Americans*. San Diego: Cabrillo Historical Assn., 1986.

Terrell, John Upton. *Journey into Darkness*. New York: William Morrow, 1962.

Wagner, Henry R. *Juan Rodríguez Cabrillo: Discoverer of the Coast of California*. San Francisco: California Historical Society, 1941.

Wepman, Dennis. *Hernán Cortés*. New York: Chelsea House, 1986.

Winsor, Justin, ed. *Spanish Exploration and Settlements in America from the Fifteenth to the Seventeenth Century*. Narrative and Critical History of America, vol. II. Boston: Houghton Mifflin, 1886.

Woods, Peter. *The Spanish Main*. Alexandria, VA: Time-Life Books, 1979.

Index

COLOPHON

This book was designed and typeset on an Apple® Macintosh SE® computer using Aldus Freehand® and Aldus PageMaker® software. The typefaces are Times and Geneva.

Other Titles from EZ Nature Books

SAN LUIS OBISPO COUNTY: A LOOK BACK INTO THE MIDDLE KINGDOM, Dan Krieger. Revised reprint. $17.95

CALIFORNIA'S CHUMASH INDIANS by Santa Barbara Museum of Natural History. $5.95

SANTA BARBARA SECRETS & SIDETRIPS by Laurie MacMillan. A guide book. $8.95

VENTURA COUNTY COMPANION by Tom Tuttle. A guide book. $8.95

BICYCLING SAN LUIS OBISPO COUNTY by Sharon Lewis Dickerson. A guide book. $6.95

MOUNTAIN BIKING THE CENTRAL COAST by Carol Berlund. A guide book. $7.95

CALIFORNIA INDIAN WATERCRAFT by Richard W. Cunningham. Water transport in California and Baja from pre-mission days to mid-19th century. $12.95

THE LIFE AND TIMES OF FRAY JUNIPERO SERRA by Msgr. Francis J. Weber. Extractions from Rev. Maynard Geiger's immense work. Revised reprint. $5.95

FROM FINGERS TO FINGER BOWLS by Helen Linsenmeyer. A lively history of California cooking from Indian days to 1900. Reprint. $14.95

HEARST'S DREAM by Taylor Coffman. How Hearst Castle came to be. $8.95

SENTINELS OF SOLITUDE by Ehlers and Gibbs. Color photos of lighthouses of the U.S. west coast. Revised reprint. $14.95

MAKING THE MOST OF SAN LUIS OBISPO COUNTY by Sharon Lewis Dickerson. $9.95

MOUNTAINS OF FIRE by Sharon Lewis Dickerson. About San Luis Obispo County's Nine Sisters—a chain of ancient volcanic peaks. $7.95

These books may be ordered from the publisher, EZ Nature Books, P.O. Box 4206, San Luis Obispo, CA 93403. For shipping, please add $1.50 for the first book and $.50 for each additional book. California residents add appropriate sales tax.